Reflections on Poetry

Reflections on Poetry

ALEXANDER GOTTLIEB BAUMGARTEN'S

*Meditationes philosophicae
de nonnullis
ad poema pertinentibus*

*Translated, with the Original Text, an Introduction,
and Notes, by*

KARL ASCHENBRENNER
and
WILLIAM B. HOLTHER

UNIVERSITY OF CALIFORNIA PRESS
Berkeley and Los Angeles: 1954

UNIVERSITY OF CALIFORNIA PRESS

BERKELEY AND LOS ANGELES

CALIFORNIA

CAMBRIDGE UNIVERSITY PRESS

LONDON, ENGLAND

PRINTED IN THE UNITED STATES OF AMERICA

BY THE UNIVERSITY OF CALIFORNIA PRINTING DEPARTMENT

L. C. CATALOG CARD NO. 54-6475

DESIGNED BY ADRIAN WILSON

Preface

ALEXANDER GOTTLIEB BAUMGARTEN has been known to students of philosophy and the theory of criticism mainly as the inventor of the term "aesthetics." His reasons for this choice of term, the meaning he attached to it, and his contribution to the philosophical study of the arts—all these have been unknown to most readers. Excerpts of the work here offered have occasionally appeared in English translation, and there is a German version by Riemann. The text itself is hard to come by, and there are not many persons who have the time or patience to struggle with the philosophical Latin of the eighteenth century. But the importance of Baumgarten in the history of aesthetics and the characteristic clarity and vigor of his thought on a subject of acknowledged difficulty have readily led us to the conclusion that his work should regain its interest if it is again made available to students of aesthetics and to general readers. We therefore offer no excuse for rescuing the *Meditationes,* Baumgarten's earliest work, from undeserved obscurity. What may need excuse is the occasional inelegance or possible inaccuracy in our effort to grasp the author's intention.

The text we reproduce is that of the first edition of 1735. This contains many errors, but it is uncertain that it would be rewarding to attempt to edit it. The two earlier printings, that by Croce in 1900, and that dedicated to him in 1936, are, like the present facsimile, mere reissuings. For the purpose of translation we have been compelled to emend the text and

[v]

not infrequently. Many errors are obvious or trivial, and we have not usually remarked them in the notes. Neither of the two previous editions nor Riemann's German translation has caught the numerous wrong propositional derivations. Some of these mistakes may be the result of a later reordering of his propositions by the author; others are certainly misprints.

Of the frequent inaccuracies in quotation, even from the chief source, Horace's *Ars poetica,* some seem owing to differences between Baumgarten's texts and ours, and others to the fact that Baumgarten, in the eighteenth-century manner, preferred to quote from memory, or to pretend to do so. In translating we have followed modern texts of the classics, without always remarking in the notes the differences, which for the most part are unimportant.

We were anticipated in the task of tracking down the citations to Horace by Riemann, who had found some, perhaps half, of them, though he seldom troubled to locate what was not right at hand in the *Ars poetica.* As to the quotations and direct citations, we believe we have caught them all, but we have not even attempted to fix all the allusions. Indeed, this would be nearly impossible, since Baumgarten's literary, as distinct from his philosophical, style is largely a stringing together of more or less apposite allusions, most of them from Horace, but many from other classical sources. We have noted only a few of the most striking of these.

We were fortunate in having always at our call the great learning of Professor William C. Helmbold. Our debt to our colleague can be indicated by the fact that he worked through the entire manuscript twice, making scores of suggestions, most of which we have adopted, and saving us from many errors. We also owe a special debt to Professor Stephen C. Pepper for encouraging and helping to further the project and to Professor Benson Mates for warm coöperation on special problems. We wish to thank Margaret Kerr Aschenbrenner for her help in the preparation of the manuscript.

K. A.

W. B. H.

Contents

[vii]

[The text, reproduced photographically
from the original edition, 1735]

Reflections on Poetry

Introduction

1. Rationalism Reconsidered

1. We neglect the later rationalists to our loss. Their views, where they are not totally ignored, are treated as errors which have been corrected by empiricist philosophy. No period in the history of thought is so regularly evaluated only in terms of clichés as the age from Leibniz to Kant. If Christian Wolff, its once famous spokesman, is still heard of, it is only as the soporific preacher of the "dogmatism" from which Hume awakened Kant. We hear of "rule-mongering" and "empty scholastic formalism." Other estimates run in the opposite direction. It is curious to find a school of thought which prided itself on the severity of its logical rigor fall to the side of the tender-minded in William James's celebrated division of the tough and tender minds.

This estimate of the rationalists is simply uninformed. Their program was neither mystical nor especially "dogmatic," but eminently scientific in intention. They put forth an extraordinary effort to perfect methods for assuring rigor in philosophical analysis. In devising their concepts they gave explicit and sensitive attention to common linguistic usage and convention, as the writings of Wolff will clearly show. They promoted no enmity between metaphysics and the findings of science and mathematics, and they pondered carefully the question raised by empiricists, whether knowledge derives from experience.

We cannot pause here to search for the causes of this misvaluation nor to supply all the evidence necessary to correct it. They are all part of the modern contempt for reason which first gathered momentum when it was said that the Enlightenment must be "overcome." It is to be noted that the history of philosophy first began as an independent branch of study with the Hegelians, who embraced the "concrete universal" and gloried in contradiction. The sober efforts of Kant's predecessors were found peculiarly "empty." Subsequent historians, even anti-Hegelians, repeated the charge with little modification. The rationalist method of philosophic inquiry and exposition, one or another variant of the *mos geometricus,* an anticipation of modern logical methods, was ridiculed as "sterile." It was, and still is, an easy and tempting step from the recognition of the formal character of logic to depreciations of this sort. As to the content of the old philosophy, the author of the *Critique of Pure Reason* was taken at his word, that he had effected nothing less than a "Copernican Revolution," and that he had superseded dogmatism and destroyed its "claims" once and for all. Like the music of the Baroque, rationalist philosophy seemed to many but another pretentious triviality of the *ancien régime*. With few exceptions the nineteenth century turned its back on it. Were such evaluations just? There is doubtless no progress of any kind without the rejection of the immediate past, but when that past is no longer an obstacle, it can be and deserves to be more equitably judged.

It is also no part of our purpose here to explore in general the positive merits of rationalism. We wish rather to justify the present attempt to draw attention to the value of a short work by one of the less-known figures of the school. Baumgarten's *Reflections* is a good example of what is valuable in the method and ideas of the school. It also marks the beginnings of an important change, as we shall presently see, in the structure of the sciences or disciplines which comprised rationalist philosophy. Beyond this it makes a lasting contribution to the analysis of the concepts it examines, reducing classical poetics to an orderly system within a space of two-score pages. Though it has never disappeared altogether from the attention of scholars, it deserves to have a broader present influence in the discussion of the problems of aesthetics.

Before we consider the method and argument of the *Reflections* we shall in this section (after a biographical note on the author) consider briefly the aims of aesthetics as Baumgarten formulated them and the importance of a reconsideration of his views at the present time.

2. Alexander Gottlieb Baumgarten was born in Berlin in 1714. In his introduction to the *Reflections,* he tells us a little about his early intellectual life. We know that he taught in the gymnasium at Berlin until he went to Halle and that he had been at Halle for some time before he offered his dissertation, the *Reflections.* As this was published in 1735, it is clear that he was just past twenty when he took his degree. It was followed by several other works, the most important being the *Aesthetica,* 1750, 1758, and the *Metaphysica,* 1739. The *Aesthetica,* an elaboration and extension of the ideas of the *Reflections,* remains as yet untranslated into a modern language. The author had not completed it when he died in 1762. He had held professorships at Halle and at Frankfurt on the Oder. He exerted a marked influence on his contemporaries both in aesthetics and in metaphysics. Kant was highly respectful toward him as a "philosophical analyst" and used his *Metaphysica* year in and year out as a textbook for his lectures. A large measure of Baumgarten's influence derived from the dissemination of his aesthetic ideas by his pupil and biographer Georg Friedrich Meier in the widely read *Anfangsgründe aller Schönen Wissenschaften,* Halle, 1748–1750.

Baumgarten's most lasting achievement is unquestionably the stimulus he gave toward the philosophical study of the arts. The *Reflections* and the *Aesthetica* might be called the charter of modern philosophical aesthetics.

3. While the term "aesthetics" is now in common use, it is of comparatively recent origin. One can point out precisely the place where it was first used, namely, the last pages of the work which is here presented. Many will know this much and little else about Baumgarten. Few will be aware of his reasons for this choice of term, or of what precisely he meant to denote by it. In its origins the term has, of course, nothing to do with "beauty." It derives from αἴσθησις, "perception," and not from any earlier word either for beauty or art. There is an important step in inference here, from perception to beauty, one that requires a considerable argument to justify. This argument is what Baumgarten sought to supply in the *Reflections* and in the *Aesthetica*. To be precise, it should be noted that there is no mention of "beauty" in the *Reflections*. The term he is explicating is "poetic," and also the term "perfection" as applied to discourse.

Aesthetics is to be the science which will investigate perception for the purpose of describing the kind of perfection which is proper to it. It will have its counterpart in the science of logic which will perform the same office for thought. Baumgarten, like Wolff and other rationalists, takes cognition to comprise a higher and a lower part, thought and perception. His originality consists in the effort to confer a certain autonomy upon the lower faculty and to formulate the principles of a science proper to it. He is not merely saying that the objects which we call beautiful are always objects of perception rather than abstractions or concepts. There would be little originality in this. His discovery is that beauty is not only perceptual, but is perception perfected. The problem lies in giving a more definite content than that of mere approval to the notion of perfection. The perfection that logic can guide us toward is the internal consistency of concepts and propositions and their compatibility with one another. The perfection that aesthetics is to exhibit is the clarity, vividness, fullness, and thematic harmony of perceptual representations.

Baumgarten's conception of the arts presupposes a larger system in which they find their place. When he surveyed the imposing structure of this system, the Leibniz-Wolffian philosophy, he found what seemed the precise place for art. This is described in § 115 of our text, with particular reference to the art of poetry. Logic heretofore has been considered the guide of the entire cognitive faculty in its search after truth. It has also been generally supposed that the cognitive faculty has a higher (intellectual) and a lower (perceptual) part. But in practice logic has been and can only be the guide of the higher part of the cognitive faculty. There must be a comparable guide for the lower part so that we may reach both intellectual perfection, that is, truth, and perceptual perfection. Turning back to an ancient page of philosophy, he finds that these ought to lie in the domains once called the noetic and the aesthetic. Poetry and the arts are aesthetic: on this occasion, at least, this statement is not a tautology. In the *Aesthetica* he elaborates more fully his plan for the new science. Its purpose is again given as the "perfection of sensate cognition," § 14.

Among the founders of rationalism, Spinoza and Leibniz showed little interest in the arts and as philosophers gave no account of them. But the early eighteenth century was an age of flourishing critical activity and saw the beginning or the renascence, in Germany, of one of the world's major literatures, and one which reversed the usual pattern by being critical before it became creative. Such interests were bound to affect reflection and speculation. Philosophical recognition was to be demanded not only for science but for poetry, the other arts, and history. This was especially true when these enterprises came to be regarded as having something other than the mere didactic value which Leibniz, for example, had been content to ascribe to them as their primary objective. The modification of the old system in accordance with the new trends is precisely the work which Baumgarten undertook, and he carried it out in an ingenious and original way. Only a mind gifted with some passion for the arts would have demanded a place for them beside science. It required boldness, too, to suggest that logic, which seemed to have such a fund of unassailable truths to its credit, should be asked to share its preceptorship of the cognitive faculty with a science that was to deal with fictions and fancies. The very name rang strange in the ears of the professors of *Weltweisheit*.

In the *Aesthetica* Baumgarten sets out to treat not only poetry but other arts as well; but references to them are fairly scarce in that work. Where he was thoroughly at home was in the world of classical poetry, as the scholia of the present work amply demonstrate. We should note also that his treatment of poetry is preëminently what we might nowadays call imagistic, and that many of the theorems of the *Reflections* can be profitably read with the visual arts in mind. His reform developed from the base of genuine response to art and not from an idle wish to tinker with the architectonic detail of Wolff's system of metaphysics. The immediate philosophical problem for him could hardly be anything other than that of reworking the prevailing system. He lived in an age that approached philosophic questions in terms of a system "of God, the world, and the soul of man," as the title to Wolff's German metaphysics put it. But there is no conflict between the system and the experience of art in Baumgarten. Apart from his slighting of arts other than poetry, he was admirably suited to the task he set himself.

The nature of Baumgarten's philosophic aim respecting the arts should thus be evident. He is concerned to establish their rightful claims in a total scheme: they are to be seen as enjoying a certain autonomy but only as the members of a system, while at the same time the system as a whole is to be regarded as deficient without just these members.

The fate of Baumgarten's views on art in the mind's total activity and on aesthetics in philosophy is too complex to be considered in detail here. Kant, always a firm but fair critic of Baumgarten's aesthetics, eventually showed the measure of the latter's influence upon him by denying in the first *Critique* the possibility of aesthetics and in the third making it a pillar of the Critical philosophy. It would be too much to claim unqualified success for Baumgarten in the demonstration of aesthetic autonomy. Croce shows strong reluctance to ascribe such success to him and insists that Vico was the first to plot accurately the proper zone of the arts. Without entering upon that controversy, we may observe that as a matter of fact no one, not even Croce himself, has as yet succeeded in this task.

4. It is true enough and trite enough that Baumgarten's theory reflects his age. This raises questions of his value for the present. Aesthetic theories of consequence have significance either of a universal or of a special character or of both. They will inevitably reflect one or more special values that are demanded of the arts in their own time. In one age it is moral advice that is foremost, in another representation of nature, in another the stirring of the emotions, and so on. Theories will reflect these and may even provide a perfectly adequate rationale for a given kind of art. On the other hand, theories seek also to universalize themselves, to claim validity for all times and all conditions. There is always some illusion in this because of the factors just noted. The inevitable irony in claiming universality and of nevertheless betraying rela-

tivity to particular time and particular condition will never, of course, discourage further effort. If we ask how we can set one theory above another, we can at least answer that some theories are able to accommodate at once a great number of factors that are either ignored or distortedly universalized by other theories. The examination of views of other times will always be in order so long as we are genuinely concerned for the truth and adequacy of our own.

Assuming that such observations are generally valid, we may ask how they apply to Baumgarten. He is aware of the place of emotion in art, but his theory is distinguished by a cognitive emphasis. Such views were not destined to remain long in favor. The rationalist enterprise to which he contributed an important component was not destined to hold firm against the romantic fury. Before the end of his century the doctrine of the supremacy of feeling, of feeling as the essence of art, was already in command. There followed an endless succession of aesthetic theories based on emotion, play, fancy, pleasure, the unconscious, the irrational, and so on. Like Baumgarten's theory, such theories were also to claim a special realm for art; but when they ran to their climactic extremes in the early twentieth century, they placed art at such a distance from man's other vital concerns, like the moral and intellectual ones, as to render it trivial, or became so hostile to these concerns as to tend toward irresponsibility and chaos. It would not be enough to say that both the emotive and the cognitive theories have each improperly universalized special values. The point is that we are still largely in the grip of one of these theories (or creeds) and need to reconsider the values of the other. It can offer us not just the rational and cognitive in place of the emotive, but also an ideal of balance and proportion between both of these.

Whatever may be said for or against Baumgarten's bias toward a cognitive theory of art, it is at any rate time to challenge the leading artistic dogma of the past two centuries, that art is and of right ought to be solely or preëminently the expression of emotion. We have arrived at the place where such a dogma is no longer obvious as a description nor wise if it is taken as advice. The challenge to such theories may be likened to one that could also be made against what is called empiricism in the parallel domain of science and the philosophy of science and knowledge. Experience is indeed an ingredient in scientific knowledge, but it is not obvious that it is central and essential in the manner of the empiricistic theories. "Expression of emotion" and "empiricism" are catchwords that may have outlived their usefulness.

2. *The Method*

5. The formal devices which Baumgarten adopts to guarantee clarity and consistency in argument will undoubtedly appear to our literary contemporaries as obstacles to this end. As we noted earlier, the romantic reaction against the Enlightenment raised numerous objections to the "empty formalism" of efforts such as this one. Literary criticism of this sort is not only beside the point; it also betrays the poverty of its understanding of the demands of clear thinking. We have to decide whether the study of literature is itself to be literature, that is, art, or whether it is to be science. There is, to be sure, room enough for both of these, but we ought to be clear that the one is not the other. The study of aesthetic matters is always beset by arbitrary demands that it somehow show as pleasing an aesthetic surface as the subject matter treated; Disappointment is expressed when an analysis of humor is not funny. No analysis is or can be identical with what is analyzed, nor will the one of necessity have the shape or color of the other. Yet, in the discussion of the arts more than anywhere else, the idea prevails that scientific treatment

or analysis destroys what is treated or analyzed. This is one of
those tender-minded, or softheaded, delusions that will probably not abate until the world decides that it cannot wait any
longer for a scientific search into the secrets of artistic pro-
duction and response. Other sciences have by now completely
forgotten their mystic beginnings. They have moved toward
clear and detailed understanding of nature. But the achievement of the artist is still bathed in mystery. Prevailing atti-
tudes toward art and the artist are akin to the wonderment of
the Psalmist at the works of God. In each of these matters,
many have seen fit to regard it as disrespectful to seek to
supplement wonder with understanding.

The method which Baumgarten employs has much in common with that which many logicians and philosophers of
science regard as the only proper method for the rigorous
exposition of the propositions of any science. Carefully followed, this method guarantees, so far as method can do so,
that we are in control of a subject, rather than its confused
victims. This is what is now known as the axiomatic method.
Where the separate truths we have about a given subject matter are not simply the record of separate observations, but are
interconnected as evidence and conclusion, this method serves
to expound these truths. But it is not only a way of ordering
what we know, showing the relevance of one proposition or
concept to another; it may also show how truths are implied
of which we were once ignorant. The vitality of the method
lies in the fact that what seems only vaguely relevant can,
with sufficient care, be shown either to take its place somewhere in the system, to follow from the assumptions, or be
summarily excluded. (There are technical qualifications to
this which we need not consider here.) We are thus in a
position to decide whether to sacrifice the assumptions or the
purported novel "truth." The "novelty" that sentimentalists
claim is not possible in such a system turns out to be logical,

not psychological, novelty. The novelty excluded is simply the irrelevant or extraneous proposition which does not follow from the assumptions. When we understand the working of the method we are in a better position to decide how we must modify our assumptions if we are to account for propositions which we find to be true.

If we employ this method at all, we must conform to its demands with absolute fidelity. Unfortunately almost all discourse in the common languages (English, German, Latin, etc.) tolerates and often flourishes on vagueness. This is glorious for poets but disastrous for scientists. No language, to be sure, is inherently vague. Everything depends upon the use to which it is put. There are, generally, far too many ambiguities in the natural languages for them to serve in their natural state as the vehicles of absolutely strict deduction. Many believe that a carefully worked out formal or "symbolic" language alone precisely answers to such a demand. However that may be, the fairest evaluation of the use in the past of the deductive method employing natural rather than "symbolic" or artificial language is obviously that it was right in its intent, a step in the right direction. We must be cautioned, in using the method, that not every subject matter may be in a condition for such treatment, though there is no rule that can tell us when the time is ripe. Many would rather see Spinoza, one of the most famous practitioners of the method, devote all his effort to the presentation of his thoughts in the noble style of his scholia and appendices. But the advantages of the method are numerous. We always know in it exactly where we are: whether a proposition is assumed without proof or not, whether a given sentence is a definition or an assertion, whether it follows from some other or not. Where there are faults, they are the faults of the practitioners, not of the method. The formidable exterior which the *Reflections* presents to the reader will probably justify these remarks.

6. In the *Reflections* we notice that some of the numbered propositions have words in capitals in the Latin, or in bold-face type in the translation. These propositions are intended as definitions of a special sort. If they are taken as "nominal definitions," which are neither true nor false, they are merely indications of how a term (the *definiendum*) is going to be used. Such usage may or may not be in accordance with common usage, if the word has one, and the statement that says that such and such a usage in the text is identical with common usage is of course either true or false. But when we say that the definitions are, nevertheless, neither true nor false, we mean that their function in the system is only that of setting up a rule of usage for the system, irrespective of usage elsewhere. As we shall see, Baumgarten's definitions are not really of this sort since he asserts their truth and makes deductions from them. Some thirty-three, or more than one-fourth, of the numbered propositions in the *Reflections* are or contain definitions. We notice also that with rare exceptions none of these thirty-three has any number cited after it. Wherever such numbers appear after propositions, or parts of propositions, they serve as references to earlier propositions which are either the definitions of the terms in the propositions in question or are premises which imply them, or both.

Speaking generally, a deductive system involves three kinds of sentential expressions:

1) *Definitions*. Sentences which indicate the meaning given to terms in the system.

2) *Axioms*. Propositions for which no previous propositions are cited as premises.

3) *Theorems*. Propositions which are implied by axioms or previous propositions or both and which are deduced from them.

In the *Reflections* we find that, strictly speaking, no proposition functions as an axiom in this sense because there are no propositions other than definitions that have no other propositions cited as premises. In other words, all propositions outside the definitions are theorems. (There are two or three minor exceptions.) But the method employed by Baumgarten requires the use of the definitions as axioms. It is always possible to replace a definition by an axiom which reads exactly the same way. The point is that if we treat a definition as an axiom we can then regard it as either true or false, and it can then take its place in the chain of deduction. If we suppose that this operation has been tacitly performed on definitions containing terms in boldface, they may be regarded as axioms and used in inferring the theorems of the system.

Even if taken as nominal, these definitions are the heart of the system, for everything else in it depends upon them. Some expressions will be defined in terms of others. For example, § 4 defines "sensate discourse" in terms of "sensate representations," a term which is defined in § 3. It is interesting to note that it is not exhaustively defined by reference to § 3, for it contains the expression "involving" by which we have translated the genitive force of *representationum sensitivarum*. One might say that a whole theory of semantics is presupposed in this genitive, which expresses the relation of sensate discourse to what discourse is about. We must also note that some of the terms in boldface will *not* be defined in terms of the others. For example, § 1 defines "discourse" as "a series of words signifying connected representations." The latter phrase is not defined elsewhere in the system. A system must begin somewhere and cannot define every term in it without remainder. The author assumes that the reader already understands the phrase, and he invites him to agree with his use of the defined terms.

But if it is necessary to treat these definitions as axioms, then, as we have said, we are not just nominally defining terms: the reader must grant the truth of the axioms, or he rejects the system *ab initio.* Of course, he is free to do this. We note again that since every system must begin somewhere it cannot prove everything without remainder.

Putting aside numerous further technical questions about the method of the *Reflections,* the issue comes down simply to whether we are prepared either to define the terms as Baumgarten has done, or, taking the definitional propositions as axioms, to accept the axioms as true. If we should, left to ourselves, define these terms in a different manner, we would nevertheless be neither agreeing nor disagreeing with him by accepting the system (if it is otherwise self-consistent). At worst we would only be allowing him to talk about a subject matter which he calls poetry but which we do not. We would not be investing any of our intellectual capital, so to speak, if we let him define mere words as he pleases. On the other hand, we do invest if we declare one of his axioms true or false, for this is a matter of agreeing or disagreeing about the nature of the thing the axiom describes. We can of course say tolerantly, Define your terms as you wish, or, Let us suppose your axioms are true, what are the results? The system as a whole shows us these results.

One of the advantages of this method is the brevity with which a large body of material can be discussed. The main part of the system is in the comparatively few numbered propositions. More diffuse material is left to the scholia. A kind of compass is thus provided that keeps the discussion channeled toward precise conclusions. Many discussions of poetry are approximately what we would have if we omitted the theorems in the *Reflections* and made a few gestures toward connecting the scholia into a continuous tale.

To achieve conciseness, the author employs still another formal device. This the translators have not been able to carry over into the English version. In most of the definitions and theorems the author has put certain words in italics to emphasize them in a very special way. When we read just the italicized words (and supply one or another form of "to be"), we get a short proposition which is a précis or the gist of the whole. For example, § 14 reads, *"Representationes distinctae completae adaequatae profundae per omnes gradus non sunt sensitivae, ergo nec poeticae."* Reading just the italicized words, we get, "Distinct representations are not poetic." Owing to the uninflected character of English and the problem of word order we have had to omit the reproduction of this ingenious device.

7. If the reader's difficulties with the *Reflections* were only those of distinguishing the kinds of propositions and the technique of deduction, they would be small indeed. One of the more serious charges against the use of the deductive method by the rationalists is that it gives only an illusion of clarity, that closer inspection reveals a profusion of unclarified notions and a tangle of non sequiturs. We may concede that the method is never perfect in anyone's hands. We need not go far in the *Reflections* to look for difficulties of this kind. The reader can ask himself how, precisely, § 5 follows from § 2 and § 4, or how the three aspects of discourse named in § 6 are derived from § 4 and § 1, and so on. If one were to study the system carefully, many more such questions would arise. But clearly all that this reveals is that the method has not been applied strictly enough. Careful analysis would show us what the "real axioms" of the system are, the assumptions that would have to be made explicit to derive the theorems as they now stand. Further analysis would show us whether they were compatible with and independent of one another.

While all this seems alien to the study of the arts as it has been carried on since the eighteenth century, there is certainly this advantage in such a method, as already noted, that in using it we always know or can easily find out exactly what it is we have assumed, and what, if anything, we have proved. The results that great but capricious minds arrive at may be just as true and far more important than anything Baumgarten arrives at, but if there is no reasoning behind them they can be but the beginnings, not the completion, of knowledge. There is nothing incompatible between the method and any truth that it may fall to the lot of anyone to discover. We may concede that there are values in the diffuse, chatty, witty insights of a critic as well as in the deductions of a theorist. Nothing illustrates this better than the *Reflections*. The author takes many of his insights from Horace's *Ars poetica,* where they are stated in the concise and concrete manner of the critic and poet, and from them or through them he derives scientific generalizations. We must forego considering the nature of this transformation here.

Once the method is second nature to the theorist he can be just as wise or witty as his gifts allow, but in using the method he takes the risk of exhibiting his possible failure in proving what he set out to prove. It is not a career that can be pursued by would-be theorists who flourish because they have mastered the arts of ambiguity and invalid inference.

As we have seen, there are many difficulties endemic to the effort to proceed by the *mos geometricus* in an unformalized language. Thought is too quick and slippery in such a tongue for us to pause long enough to see whether something "follows." But as things stand, such efforts as Spinoza's *Ethics,* various works of Leibniz, and the Latin works of Wolff are certainly among the most determined efforts ever put forth to think consecutively and rigorously on nonmathematical subject matters in an unformalized language. Baumgarten's *Reflections* exhibits all the dangers and all the benefits of following their example.

3. The Argument

8. The problem which Baumgarten sets himself is to define the specific differences which distinguish poetic from other discourse and to examine with all the precision possible the attributes which, as he says, "contribute to the perfection of a poem." While he wants to do this within the conceptual framework of his school, he is prepared to by-pass the scholastic constructions of the "Scaligers and Vosses" and draw directly on the great classical tradition of poetics. He goes not, as one might expect, to Aristotle, but to Horace. Aristotle was chiefly interested in drama, while Horace, a practicing (and reflecting) poet, attempted to apply the "imitation of an action" and some other by then time-honored constructions to a wider range of poetry. Perhaps Baumgarten's choice of Horace merely illustrates the fondness of the century for the Odes and Satires, which he has by heart.

The insights of the *Ars poetica* (henceforth to be referred to simply as "*A.P.*") are familiar to most students of aesthetics. They take the form of advice to the would-be poet to choose certain (and avoid certain other) subjects; ways of beginning, developing, and treating; devices of style; kinds of diction; means for obtaining vividness. Most of this advice is quite familiar from earlier sources. When Horace says that tragic writers should stick to well-known names and situations (*A P.* 119–131), we recall Aristotle's observation (*Poetics,* 1451b15) that, as something that has actually happened is obviously possible, retelling the stories of the famous heroes conforms to the law of probability and necessity—or, as we should say, verisimilitude. Horace is not slavish. Aristotle's famous requirement of a beginning, middle, and end (*Poetics* 1450b25) is given a witty twist, without perhaps a real change of sense, in Horace's advice that a poem begin *in medias res,*

that is, in the middle (*A.P.* 148). This is no doubt in the
interest of poetic condensation.

Horace, after all, was preparing a sort of poetic distillation
of classical poetics. The *Ars poetica* is more than a treatise on
poetics; it is a brilliant poem illustrating many of the things
it talks about, so it is not surprising that it is not always sufficiently lucid (even on the subject of lucidity, see *Reflections,*
§ 73) to suit the scientific interests of Baumgarten. Instead of
rejecting Horace's criticism as wrongheaded and nonsensical,
Baumgarten turns to the practice in this poem and others to
supplement the maxims, and seeks to make his own kind of
sense out of it. The situation is rather like that which might
prevail if a student of Charles Morris should undertake to see
what could be done with the chaotically articulate criticism
of Auden and Eliot in the light of their best poems. To
borrow a phrase from Reichenbach, Baumgarten is attempt-
ing a "rational reconstruction," not of physical science, to be
sure, but of criticism, and that instance of it which is in the
best taste available. He perfectly understands what he is
doing. When the meta-science he is employing has for its
object, as in the present work, the criticism of poetry (that is,
poetics), he calls this science "philosophical poetics" (§ 9).
When the field is broadened to include the criticism of all the
arts, he coins for it the name "aesthetics" (§ 115, § 116).

It is something of an achievement that Baumgarten is able
to discover a coherent poetics in the bits of Horatian wisdom
and rules of thumb, or to invent one from them. He spreads
them out and weaves them together by relating them,
through definitions and axioms, to fundamental clear and
distinct principles; two such principles. One he finds in
Horace; this is the concept of "lucid order," which is sufficiently vague in the source to tolerate considerable interpretation. The other is got by a novel employment of a basic notion
of rationalism, familiar to students as the doctrine of "clear

and distinct ideas." Before discussing poetic order, we shall
have to see what it is that is ordered by it. In the next section,
then, we shall want to see how Baumgarten is able to ration-
alize the traditional poetics of subject matter and style by
means of the theory of ideas inherited from Descartes,
Leibniz, and Wolff.

9. It is well known that the great rationalists tried to base
their demonstrations on what they called "clear and distinct
ideas." Reason was to be the ultimate test of truth, and it thus
becomes important to find out what this test is. Now we form
ideas of things from our senses. Such ideas may be either clear
or obscure. Other creatures, animals and perhaps even plants,
if they form them at all, form relatively obscure ideas. Though
our own ideas may differ only in degree from these, it is
possible for the senses to form very clear ideas.

Since poetry occurs in discourse, Baumgarten speaks of
representations rather than ideas, representations being ideas
expressed in language. Representations formed by the poet
will have to be clear. If he wishes to convey the idea of love,
for example, he may find that the apprehension of this state
is very obscure (and confused, too). He must find clear representations for it or he will fail to communicate. Poetry is
intended to communicate (scholium to § 12), and only clear
representations can be distinguished from each other and
sufficiently recognized to serve for communication (§ 13).
We shall in a moment see what kind of clarity is available to
the poet.

Now though the clarity of ideas which man derives from
sense may be superior only in degree to the clarity of ideas
which animals have, we are in a privileged position compared
with the rest of mortal creation in having another way to
form ideas than through the senses. When we recognize something—Leibniz's example is gold (*Discourse on Metaphysics,*

and reaches out in all sorts of directions which the sterner faculty, with its eye on the essence, would find accidental and irrelevant.

We should say today that the ideal poetic representation is a highly condensed symbol, rich with ambiguity and as complex as the poet can contrive. In Baumgarten's terms, the more a representation embraces, the more extensive clarity it has. While it avoids the kind of exclusions required for distinctness—it makes its own kind of exclusions in the interest of brevity, as we shall presently see—and while it embraces a lifelike manifold of external properties, it still serves all the more sharply to particularize its object. Completely particularized representations are those of individuals: these are in the highest degree poetic. Thus extensive clarity insures that our representations will be vivid with sensuous detail and at the same time fully concrete (§§ 16–20). In fact, the sensuous detail is what makes them concrete. The detail may not be logically necessitated—poets are not interested in scientific classification and the discernment of distinct and fundamental traits. But poetry will realize its object in a very determinate way.

The poet is interested in being specific—this is his kind of clarity—and in the economy to be had only by fusing categories. Baumgarten quotes Horace's odes to show how the poet employs such expressions as "old Massic" for any well-aged wine and how he adduces particular instances for the most general concepts, such as avarice (§ 20). To be particular and specific—this is why poets are fond of examples, since examples are the representations of something more specific supplied to clarify the representations of something less specific (§ 21). This is also why poets like the representation of complex rather than simple things, of wars rather than, say, headaches (§ 23).

Poetic principles, most of them from Horace's advice or

practice, are now introduced as falling under the principle of extensive clarity. It is highly poetic to represent very affecting situations, since the affects (how things appear to us as good or bad) are something added and thus extend the representation (§§ 25–27). Poets employ images, sometimes perhaps too freely, but so far as images are sensate they are poetic. They are economical as well: when partially represented, the image of the object will recur as a whole; this is why poets successfully employ images of time and season (§§ 28–35). Casual resemblances; even dreams and sensuous memories (§§ 37–42); representations of wonders, provided there is something familiar mingled in them (§§ 44–47); miracles, although "nature has certainly nothing to do with miracles" (§ 49); that kind of images called fictions, if they are not absolutely impossible ("utopian" is the sarcastic designation of fictions, such as of adulterous gods, that we know to be "impossible in all possible worlds") and if they are consistent and plausible (§§ 52–59); descriptions, by which the poet can pleasantly fuse together sense impressions, images, and fictions (§§ 54–55); previsions of the future and prophecies, especially if the outcome is already fully specified (has occurred in fact), as when Horace has Nereus predict the outcome of the Trojan War (§§ 60–65)—all these devices are available to the poet for extending the scope of his representations and thus achieving the clarity of vivid and concrete detail.

The poetics of extensive clarity is, then, the poetics of the concrete and vivid. The author says as much. The vivid characterizes discourse in which we are led to perceive details (§ 112). Baumgarten is at some pains to show that this notion of the vivid is consistent with common usage. It rather well sums up the "extensive" part of extensive clarity.

There is no difficulty for this poetics in explaining the function of figurative usage: it contributes to vividness and

concreteness. Baumgarten's way of saying this is rather formidable, as he wishes to employ only terms fully defined in the
system. The representations which approach a thing through
a figure are sensate and thus belong to that part of discourse
to which poetry belongs; furthermore, figurative terms supply
complex confused representations in abundance. Thus they
are poetic on two counts (§ 79). They have an added advantage. When the poet must introduce non-sensate conceptions,
say an abstraction like tenderness, he is able by means of a
figure to reduce the conception to concrete images. The alter-
native would be to think the abstraction through to distinctness, as in a psychological analysis of the emotion, a process
which is nonpoetic (§ 80). Metaphors, among the figures,
have still another poetic quality. They exploit resemblances
which (as one learns in § 30) are a poetic way to achieve
greater extensive clarity (§ 83). The result is not guaranteed,
however, and some figurative usages might tend to obscurity
(§ 83), a possibility in all sensate representation.

The point here is worth noting. Representations of the
identical thing "can be to one person obscure, to another clear,
to a third even distinct," but what is under discussion is the
representations *intended* by the poet (§ 12). If these are sensate, we have seen that they may be either clear or obscure.
Some poets, in their figurative and other employments, exhibit a taste for the obscure. As Baumgarten says, they think
"the more obscure and intricate their effusions, the more
'poetic' their diction." They are wrong. A poem is a perfected
form of sensate discourse, and in discourse one intends to
communicate his representations. As we have seen (p. 19
above), only clear representations can be communicated.

Figurative usage is correctly understood here, not as a
mere embellishment of "purple patches" (*A.P.* 14 f.), but as
central to poetic practice. It is not certain that Baumgarten
can accommodate metrics so plausibly. Words are sounds and

as such elicit sense perceptions (§ 78 and § 91). Thus sounds lead to confused judgments of pleasure or pain (§ 92). So far as either the pain or pleasure is marked in degree, under the rules we have a poetic situation: since these confused judgments are sensate, they are poetic (§ 93), the more marked, the more poetic (§ 94). How does Baumgarten exclude the painful? The painful, he says (§ 95), will distract the attention of the listener, and the poem will fail in its purpose to communicate. Whatever one thinks of this, the author is now ready to discuss such of the elements of sonority and metrics as the young schoolmaster in him inclines to instruct us in. So far as verses produce pleasure in the sense of hearing, they are by rule poetic.

The author avoids the mistake of regarding the control of the sound as the ultimate perfection by which we can make poetry out of nonpoetic but otherwise perfected sensate discourse. If verse does not make the poem, what does? Not even entirely concrete and vivid representations make a poem, though without them there can be no poem. It is a fair summary of many propositions to state that they are designed to make explicit that whatever contributes in any way toward making discourse characteristically sensate is in some degree poetic: it is the raw material of a poem. But there is another element to discourse, in addition to words and representations, and this must also be perfect if discourse is to achieve the highest degree of perfection. It is the interconnection of the representations. In one place Baumgarten says, "It is the interconnection that is poetic" (§ 68). We have seen something of the kind of material a poem deals with—representations fused together and rendered as vivid and concrete as possible. It is time now to turn to the interconnections, the method by which the clear and confused representations are ordered in the poem.

10. Confused and extensively clear representations are characteristic of all perfected sensate discourse, and a poem, by definition (§ 9), is a perfected instance of sensate discourse. This poses a problem of distinguishing a poem from other instances in the same genus—a problem of specific differences. The control of sound, we have seen, is not sufficient. The author believes, we have suggested, that the distinguishing characteristic lies in the concept of lucid order.

Baumgarten allows that the difference between the perfection of poetry and of the rhetorical forms of discourse is a matter of degree (§ 117). Yet he believes that, of all the forms of sensate discourse, only a poem can be entirely perfect. Though the difference is a matter of degree, there must also be a difference in kind in order to insure poetry its preëminence. The author does not make this argument explicit, and, indeed, it is not a necessary consequence of any proposition or set of propositions. It is implicit in the discussion of order. In considering the kind of organization that Baumgarten, following Horace, regards as characteristic of good poetry, we can best begin by noting the preparation for the introduction of the concept of lucid order.

One has learned early in the *Reflections* that sensate discourse is not merely a series of discrete representations, however clear. Discourse comes organized: there are interconnections (§ 6). Now one learns (§ 66) that all organized discourse is discourse the parts of which are subordinated to a theme. In defining the "theme," Baumgarten introduces, as a primitive concept, Leibniz's principle of sufficient reason: the "theme" is that which in representation contains the sufficient reason of other representations in the discourse, but which does not find its own sufficient reason in them. We note that the definition of a theme can apply also to other kinds of organized discourse besides poetry.

From the definition of the theme, the author can easily

deduce the consequence that there can be only one theme, if the alleged themes are connected (§ 67). And they must be connected, as interconnection contributes to the perfection of sensate discourse (§ 65) and whatever does so is poetic (§ 7, § 11). There is the further consequence that all other elements should be subordinate to the theme; otherwise, they would be unconnected, hence unpoetic (§ 68).

Every sense impression, every image must be determined through the theme, for the poetry lies in the interconnections. This, says Baumgarten, will put a "curb" to the "wits," who might want to "abuse the previous propositions, where we not only admitted images and fictions into a poem but assumed their perfection." Such representations may be independently good, but in their coördination "every sense idea, every depiction, every fantasy ... which does not conform to the design" (*A.P.* 195) must be excluded. What the author expects of the poet is conveyed in an important but somewhat cryptic remark. The poet is like a creator, and the poem like a little world, and we ought to think of it what "is evident to the philosophers concerning the real world" (§ 68).

With all representations subordinated to the theme, they will be interconnected among themselves by sufficient reasons, like causes and effects. If this is accomplished, there is order in the poem (§ 69). Order in a succession of representations is called "method." When we speak of poetic method, we are to follow Horace and call it "lucid" (*A.P.* 41, § 70).

Baumgarten is now ready to lay down "the general rule of lucid method." It is, simply stated, a method by which poetic representations progressively reveal the theme (§ 71). Later representations must set forth the theme of the poem more clearly than the earlier ones. Continuing the thought of the scholium to § 68, he elaborates the comparison between the poet and the Creator. There is an analogy, he says, "in the rule of order by which things in the world follow one another

for disclosing the glory of the Creator, the ultimate and highest theme of some immense poem, if one may so speak"
(scholium to § 71).

Such is the general rule. Evidently certain exclusions will
operate. It is not surprising to learn, for example, that certain
elements ought to be omitted from a poem. If we should try
to present every interconnection of a historical theme, we
might end with all the history of all the ages (§ 76). We are
advised to be brief. Baumgarten's definition of "brevity" is
simple: intrinsic or absolute brevity is leaving out whatever
can be left out without the loss of a degree of perfection
(§ 74). These considerations apply to all discourse. In particular, the author continues, "such brevity, since it is proper
to every discourse, is also proper to a poem."

In the light of this, the author is perhaps altogether too
brief in his treatment of the special methods of poetic exposition. Two propositions deserve close attention. One tells us
that there are three ways in which representations can
"cohere." They are (a) as premises with conclusion, the
method corresponding to this being the method of reason;
(b) as like with like and related with related, the method
corresponding being the method of wit, and (c) through
the law of sensation and imagination, the method corresponding being the method of memory (§ 72). The other immediately advises us that if one of these methods contradicts a
poetic rule, such as the rule of progressive realization of the
theme, we can "go over from one method to another" (§ 73).
The scholium to this proposition shows its importance. The
author quotes Horace to the effect that the poet will say right
now what must now be said and put off whatever follows
from another order of thought. "We may concede that
Horace had no *distinct* conceptions either of lucid method
or any other, but there ought to be no doubt about the true
sense." Yet there is some doubt, since we are told so little of

how the poet employs the three methods (of reason, wit, and memory).

In the final section (after the author has done with figures and metrics) there is further discussion of various aspects of poetic order and method. The first is a definition of "imitation." To imitate something, we learn, is to make something similar to it. Hence an effect similar to something can be said to be an imitation of it, even if it is achieved unintentionally (§ 108). Baumgarten proceeds: "If a poem is regarded as an imitation of nature or of actions, its effects must be similar to those produced by nature" (§ 109). Though representations produced immediately from nature can never be distinct and intelligible (since they are sensate), they can be extensively clear and hence poetic. Nature and the poet create resemblances. Hence the poem is an imitation of nature (§ 110). In this proposition representations produced immediately from nature are also described as arising "from the intrinsic principle of change in the universe and from actions dependent on this." We know that the poem resembles nature in the way nature progressively manifests her theme. But we are given no further clarification of the "actions" of nature which the poem imitates. They are presumably the exfoliation of substance into individual, the endless repetition of general types with subtle individual differences, the progressive movement of the causal series, the constant creation at each successive moment of time of the best possible and the greatest possible number of things, in accordance with the principle of sufficient reason. These are metaphysical matters, and the author is exempt from discussing them, but his parallels between the world and the poem show that he has them in mind.

Despite the difficulty of these passages, we can see that the author's representational theory of poetic organization is a theory of the imitation of nature in a novel and ingenious sense: the poem is a "representation" not only of objects and events in the world, but of the processes of creation. If we ask how the poet is able to imitate so creatively, we note, first, that the activity need not be deliberate, and second, that there is more than one method or rule that the poet can employ and that he can shift from one to another. The rule Baumgarten chooses for illustration is the rule of progressively manifesting the theme, an activity in which the poem so closely resembles nature that he speaks, as we saw, of the order in the world, by which the things that happen one after the other progressively manifest the glory of the Creator as the theme of some immense poem (§ 71).

Even when we allow for all these devices of poetic practice, we may yet ask for a still more specific difference between poetry and other forms of sensate discourse. We recall that the author set himself this task in the early propositions of the *Reflections*. The poem is indeed a "bounded" discourse, but beyond this, he implies, no further difference may ever be found; let the discourse be sufficiently perfected, and we can, if we choose, regard it as poetry. The difference then will be, as the author says, a matter of degree (§ 117). This is a remarkable result in a day before free verse could have been thought poetry at all. Even in these late decades of the modern poetry movement, not many look for the poetic quality in progressively clearer manifestations of the theme through increasingly vivid and concrete representations. We are still prone to think it lies in the available form or in the fashionable diction or in the preferred stock of images and themes. We need to make certain rediscoveries about poetic values and methods. The *Reflections* can be of the greatest value in reminding us of what once was demanded of a poet and may again be.

11. We may note finally that Baumgarten, without explicitly invoking the ancient critical division of form and con-

tent, has in remarkably few words set forth the essence of both these concepts and provided many useful clues to their application. He has achieved this principally by his expositions of the doctrines of clear and confused representations, of the theme, and of imitation. Later aestheticians have poured out abuse on the notion of imitation because it seemed antithetical to artistic creativity. Baumgarten seeks to reconcile imitation and creation by appropriating the rationalist metaphysics of natural process and the prevailing religious views about the grand design of an Author of Nature as metaphors to describe the artist's effort. Nature as process, *natura naturans* in Spinoza's phrase, develops in time. To the eye of faith it moves toward "one far-off divine event." Just so the poet must work toward one "event," the theme. He must exploit to the fullest measure, with appropriate material and by formal means, every moment the reader devotes to him. Every part must be intrinsically interesting, arresting. This is achieved by the richness and vividness of the character of each event and place and person. But every part must also lead to the next part, to the end, and it must belong to the whole. This is achieved by relation to a theme, one theme. The parts gain relation from one point to any other only by their common relation to a central point. Of every part of a poem, and, by extension, of every work of art, we may ask why this part is present rather than absent. We may ask, in other terms, in the terms of the rationalists, for the sufficient reason of every part. Only a theme can serve as a sufficient reason, for it alone is self-sufficient. The theme is revealed only in the whole career of the poem in time. Since it is self-sufficient, there can be no more than one theme in a poem.

Form, or the interrelation of parts, we must note, is not for Baumgarten an external, intellectual thing. It is itself poetic. That is to say, it must again be grasped in clear and confused representations. There is actually no difficulty in this.

Our terms for relation are often represented by philosophers as intellectual, where this is thought to exclude the concrete and sensuous. But every relation that any artist can exploit can be grasped in perception or imagination even if it has also an intellectual analogue. Thus, the rationalists would say that the circle can be set forth as a clear and distinct idea by a formula in analytic geometry. But it is also the unique shape the eye beholds. There is no conceivable conflict between these two, as romantic critics have falsely supposed. For if we choose to think of two circles here, intellectual and sensuous, the one can in no sense obscure or displace the other, for the clear and distinct, the intellectual, "circle" can never actually appear in any "place" whatever.

Baumgarten pursues the ideal of scientific clarity about art. In the apparent paradox of rationalism he seeks distinct ideas about a confused subject matter. He seeks also a proper and congenial place in the system of thought not only for mathematics and mechanics but also for what he taught us to call "aesthetics." Since science and art cannot conflict, each shall prosper.

Reflections on Poetry

.

Reflections on Poetry

FROM my earliest boyhood a certain branch of study attracted me[1] very much. There was, besides, the advice, which it is good to follow, of wise men that this study ought never to be neglected. I have now prepared myself in it to make public trial of whatever powers I may have.

Since the time when the worthy co-rector of the gymnasium which flourishes at Berlin, the celebated Christgau,[2] whom I cannot name without a sense of the deepest gratitude, adroitly guided my first steps in the study of the humanities, scarcely a day has passed for me without verse. As I grew older, my attention turned more and more to the sterner studies appropriate to the upper forms at school, until at length the academic life seemed to require other labors and other interests. Nevertheless, I addressed myself to the necessary studies in such a way that I never entirely renounced poetry, which I valued highly, as much for pure enjoyment as for its manifest usefulness.

Meanwhile, by divine will, which I honor, it happened that duty required me to tutor young men preparing for the university, in poetics, along with so-called Rational Philosophy. What in such a situation was more reasonable than, at the first opportunity, to translate our philosophical precepts into practice? What, indeed, is more unworthy of, or more difficult for, a philosopher than to swear allegiance to another man's formulas, to declaim in ringing tones the precepts of one's teachers? By way of preparation I set to work to reconsider all those things which I had learned in the usual way and by the traditional method, through practice, or by imitation—if not blind, at least one-eyed—and by watching out for other possible sources of error.

While I was busy at this, my affairs took yet another turn. With dazzled eyes, I was drawn into the light of the Fridericiana [University of Halle]. Now I vigorously reject the rashness of those who openly publish any sort whatever of crude and unpolished stuff, who prostitute the unprofitably sedulous industry of their pens to the learned world rather than honestly earn its esteem. I confess that it is for this reason that I have not sooner done justice to the obligation which the hallowed rules of academic life have laid upon me. That I may now satisfy this obligation, I have chosen a subject which many, to be sure, hold to be too trifling and remote to deserve the attention of philosophers. Yet it seems to me sufficiently serious for my slight powers and, in proportion to its dignity, well enough adapted to the exercise of minds which make the rational investigation of everything their business.

I intend to demonstrate that many consequences can be derived from a single concept of a poem which has long ago been impressed on the mind, and long since declared hundreds of times to be acceptable, but not once proved. I wish to make it plain that philosophy and the knowledge of how to construct a poem, which are often held to be entirely antithetical, are linked together in the most amiable union. To this end, through § 11 I shall be occupied in developing the notion of a poem and the appropriate terminology. From § 13 to § 65 I shall try to work out some view of poetic cognition. From § 65 to § 77 I shall set forth that lucid method of a poem which is common to all poems. Finally, from § 77 to § 107 I shall subject poetic language to a rather careful investigation. After I have in this way exhibited the fruitfulness of my definition, I regard it proper to compare it with some others and to add at the end a few words about poetics in general.

The plan of procedure has not allowed more, and the feeble-
ness of the practitioner has not permitted better. Later on,
perhaps, weightier and riper reflections will be granted by
God, time, and effort.

§ 1. By **discourse** we shall understand a series of words which
designate connected representations.

We need only appeal to this well-established word [*oratio*]
if anyone should contend that all definitions of clear terms
are superfluous. Even children understand what it is.[3] Yet
unless a distinct meaning, which we adhere to, is given a
word, the unguided mind hesitates and utterly fails to see
what meaning or force it should attribute to the word in a
given case. Prayer [*oratio*] with meditation and close attention the theologian commends; but in this use, extraneous
terms are brought into the definition of the mode. A proposition [*oratio*] the logician of the schools, following his
Aristotle, regards as "the discourse for external utterance"[4]
and defines it as that whose parts taken separately have
meaning—if his liver bothers him he demands also to know
whether a syllogism is to be considered one proposition or
several. Speech [*oratio*], the rhetor loudly proclaims, is to
be rigorously distinguished from declamation, if we are to
avoid the appearance of confusing battles with games. Let
those who follow the common usage of language dig out
what that may be which we nowadays call "discourse" in
the larger sense: if anybody prefers to call it "speech"
[*sermo*] we shall not wage a war which would bring no
victory. He who thinks of the *Sermones* of Horace will see
that it is better to avoid that term here.

§ 2. Connected representations are to be apprehended from
discourse, § 1.

The axiom of the definition [§ 1] is the minor premise; the
definition of "significance" or "sign" will give the major,

which is left out here as sufficiently familiar in ontology.[5]
We ask leave to advance without demonstration (while
keeping this in view) that which clearheaded philosophers
hold to be demonstrated and defined without further definition. Hypothetical citation of premises is inadequate. For
one thing, the evidence would have to be introduced from
another quarter; for another, connection could be established only by transference to another type of argument.[6]
Cicero says, "Nevertheless, such is the custom of mathema-
ticians, not of philosophers. For when geometers wish to
establish anything, if any relevant matter has been exam-
ined before, they assume it as conceded and proved (defined) and set forth only that which has not already been
explained. But whatever philosophers have in hand, they
bring to bear on it everything they can, even if it has been
in dispute elsewhere."[7] Truly high praise and ample reward
for the geometryless[8] sages.

§ 3. By **sensate representations** we mean representations received through the lower part of the cognitive faculty.

Since desire, so far as it derives from a confused representation of the good,[9] is called sensate, and since, on the other
hand, a confused representation, along with an obscure one,
is received through the lower part of the cognitive faculty,
we can apply the same name to confused representations,
in order that they may be distinguished from concepts distinct at all possible levels.

§ 4. By **sensate discourse** we mean discourse involving sensate representations.

Just as no philosopher attains to such profundity that he
can see through all things, aided only by pure intellect,
without becoming entangled somewhere or other in confused thinking, so, too, practically no discourse can be so

purely scientific and intellectual that no sensate idea at all occurs in the whole context. Likewise, if one is especially looking for evidences of distinct thinking, one may find distinct representations here and there in sensate discourse; yet the discourse remains sensate, as the other remains abstract and intellectual.

§ 5. Connected sensate representations are to be apprehended from sensate discourse, § 2, § 4.

§ 6. The various parts of sensate discourse are: (1) sensate representations, (2) their interrelationships, (3) the words, or the articulate sounds which are represented by the letters and which symbolize the words, § 4, § 1.

§ 7. By **perfect sensate discourse** we mean discourse whose various parts are directed toward the apprehension of sensate representations, § 5.

§ 8. A sensate discourse will be the more perfect the more its parts favor the awakening of sensate representations, § 4, § 7.

§ 9. By **poem** we mean a perfect sensate discourse, by **poetics** the body of rules to which a poem conforms, by **philosophical poetics** the science of poetics, by **poetry** the state of composing a poem, and by **poet** the man who enjoys that state.

For rehashing these scholastic terms by nominal definitions, the overstuffed cupboards of the Scaligers, the Vosses,[10] and many others are there to be pilfered. No matter how ready we may be to dig into this, we will hold off if we take heed of this one thing: Nonius Marcellus, Aphthonius, and Donatus seem, with Lucilius,[11] to distinguish "poem" and "poetry" only quantitatively. A poem is for them some part or section of poetry, that is, of a larger poem, so that a poem and poetry differ about in the way that in Homer the *Iliad*

differs from the catalogue of the Greek ships. But Voss
holds up against these authorities the fact of usage
> *In whose power lie the decision, the rule, and the pattern
> of language.*[12]

But when he concedes that Cicero uses "poetry" in place of
"poem," he will scarcely command everyone's assent, for
the cited passages seem to suggest the contrary. When Cicero attributes to Homer the art, not of poetry, but of painting, he marvels at the ability of a blind man to imitate
everything, even that which comes through the eyes. But
he does not exclaim, at least not exclusively, over the effect
of this art, as he ought to do if the unusual meaning of the
term "poetry" could be justified from this citation. The
other passage of Cicero is to be found not in book VI of the
Tusculan Disputations, as we read in both editions of Voss,
but in book IV, where Cicero says that all Anacreon's poetry
is love poetry. Still, it is not very hard to decide, unless I am
mistaken, whether here one can properly substitute the
term "poem" in the singular [for "poetry"], or whether
Cicero is not rather saying that all the impetus behind the
outpourings of poetry in Anacreon is solely directed toward
celebrating love—and "poetry" retains its force completely
vindicated.[13]

§ 10. The several parts of a poem are: (1) sensate representations, (2) their interrelationships, (3) words as their signs,
§ 9, § 6.

§ 11. By **poetic** we shall mean whatever can contribute to the
perfection of a poem.

§ 12. Sensate representations are parts of the poem, § 10, and
hence poetic, § 11, § 7, but since sensate representations may
be either obscure or clear, § 3, poetic representations are either
obscure or clear.

Of course, representations of an identical thing can be to one person obscure, to another clear, to a third even distinct. But seeing that the discussion concerns the representations intended to be designated in discourse, we mean those representations which the speaker intends to communicate. Thus we investigate here those representations which the poet intends to designate in the poem.

§ 13. In obscure representations there are not contained as many representations of characteristic traits as would suffice for recognizing them and for distinguishing them from others, and as, in fact, are contained in clear representations (by definition). Therefore, more elements will contribute to the communication of sensate representations if these are clear than if they are obscure. A poem, therefore, whose representations are clear is more perfect than one whose representations are obscure, and clear representations are more poetic than obscure ones, § 11.

This should take care of those who wrongly suppose that the more obscure and intricate their effusions the more "poetic" their diction. We certainly do not want to go over to the opinion of those who reject the finest poets, no matter who, because they decide that in them they see, with their rheumy eyes, pure darkness and thick night. For example, Persius says,

If, overcautious, you pound down the well cap with many a plank, you will have given the people thirsty ears in vain.[14]

Only someone ignorant of Neronian history will be so rash as to brand this as Cimmerian darkness. Whoever consults that history will either arrive at the sense and experience sufficiently clear representations, or he knows no Latin.

§ 14. Distinct representations, complete, adequate, profound through every degree, are not sensate, and, therefore, not poetic, § 11.

The truth of this will become evident *a posteriori* by an experiment. Suppose we read to a man trained in philosophy and at the same time not entirely a stranger to poetry little verses overladen with distinct representations, for example:

> *Refutation is the proof that others err.*
> *No one refutes unless he proves thereby*
> *Another's fallacy. But if you want to prove*
> *Such things, it's clear you have to study logic.*
> *When you refute, you're sure to get it wrong*
> *If you are no logician—by verse one.*[15]

He will scarcely let the verses go unchallenged though they are perfect in versification. Perhaps he himself will not know for what reason they seem worthless to him, as there is nothing to criticize either in form or in content. This is the principal reason why philosophy and poetry are scarcely ever thought able to perform the same office, since philosophy pursues conceptual distinctness above everything else, while poetry does not strive to attain this, as falling outside its province. If a man excels in each part of the faculty of understanding and can employ each at will in its proper sphere, he will certainly apply himself to the exercise of the one without detriment to the other. He will see that Aristotle and Leibniz and hundreds of others who added the mantle of the sage to the laurel of the poet were prodigies, not freaks.

§ 15. Since poetic representations are clear representations, § 13, and since they will be either distinct or confused, and since they are not distinct, § 14, therefore, they are confused.

§ 16. When in representation A more is represented than in B, C, D, and so on, but all are confused, A will be said to be **extensively clearer** than the rest.

> We have had to add this restriction so that we may distinguish these degrees of clarity from those, already sufficiently understood, which, through a discrimination of characteristics, plumb the depths of cognition and render one representation *intensively clearer* than another.

§ 17. In extensively very clear representations more is represented in a sensate way than in those less clear, § 16; therefore, they contribute more to the perfection of a poem, § 7. For this reason extensively clearer representations are especially poetic, § 11.

§ 18. The more determinate things are, the more their representations embrace. In fact, the more that is gathered together in a confused representation, the more extensive clarity the representation has, § 16, and the more poetic it is, § 17. Therefore, for things to be determined as far as possible when they are to be represented in a poem is poetic, § 11.

§ 19. Individuals are determined in every respect. Therefore, particular representations are in the highest degree poetic, § 18.

> Our tyro poets,[16] far from observing this nicety of a poem, turn up their noses at Homer, who tells in *Iliad* II of the
> > *Leaders and chieftains, commanders of ships, and all the fleet.*[17]
>
> In VII he tells the stories of all those who crossed Hector's path. In the Hymn to Apollo he lists the many places sacred to the god. Likewise, in Virgil's *Aeneid*, anyone who reads through book VII and following will have many opportunities to observe the same thing. We may also cite, in the

Metamorphoses of Ovid, the enumeration of the dogs who rend their master to shreds.[18] I do not think anybody can suppose that those things which would be very difficult for us to imitate come into being without study and effort.

§ 20. Since specific determinations applied to a genus establish the species, and since generic determinations establish the inferior genus under the superior, the representations of the species and of the inferior genus are more poetic than those, respectively, of the genus or of the superior genus, § 18.

So as not to seem to drag in a farfetched proof *a posteriori,* let us cite the first Ode of Horace. If there were no merit in putting narrower concepts for broader ones, why, then, in this poem "great-grandsires" for ancestors, "Olympic dust" for the dust of the Games fields, "the palm" for the prize, "Libyan threshing-floors" for productive countries, "the circumstances of Attalus" for affluence, "Cyprian beam" for a trading ship, "Myrtoan sea" for a dangerous sea, "Africus struggling against the Icarian floods" for the wind, "Old Massic" for a well-aged wine, "the Marsian boar" for a destructive animal, and so on? We shall say nothing of the ordering of the whole ode, how, by a careful design, in place of ambition, avarice, and pleasure particular instances are introduced in which these usually discover themselves. In every development things are so specified that, where many similar cases are to be grouped under a general heading, one is exhibited and then the next.[19] See verses 26, 27, 33, 34. Likewise, Tibullus asks that three kinds of aromatics be poured on his ashes, instead of simply perfumes:

> *The wares which rich Panchaia and the eastern Arabias and fat Assyria send there* (§ 19)—*let tears mindful of me be poured into the same flask.*[20]

Instead of "I shall never do this," Virgil would be likely to say in the characteristic paraphrasis of poets,

Before that, everything will come about which I denied could happen, and things will go contrary to the laws of nature.[21]

In the first Eclogue, he proceeds to a particular enumeration of things physically impossible, in a manner especially characteristic of rustics:

Before this comes about, light stags will pasture in the sky.[22]

From this same source flows poetic distribution: when poets tend to speak of a number of things, they habitually assign them at once to classes and species. There is a well-known passage in Virgil about the Trojans driven onto the shores of Libya, in *Aeneid* I.[23] Likewise in Catullus, when the poet wishes to represent the Satyrs and Sileni of Nyssa, he says,

Some of them were waving thyrsi with covered points...,
and in the following eight verses he narrates several kinds of activity.[24]

§ 21. By **example** we mean a representation of something more determined which is supplied to clarify the representation of something less determined.

Since I have not seen this definition elsewhere, in order to show that it accords perfectly with accepted usage I may refer to the arithmetician who asserts that equal quantities added to equal produce an equal aggregate, or, if $A = Z$, $B = Y$, then $A + B = Z + Y$. If he substitutes the determinate number 4 in the place of the undetermined number A; in place of Z, $2 + 2$; in place of B, 6; in place of Y, $3 + 3$; and asserts that $4 + 6 = 2 + 2 + 3 + 3$, everyone will say that he has given an example for his axiom, because the substitution was made for the purpose of showing more clearly what he intended by the letters. Suppose a philosopher wants to demonstrate that nonproper locutions[25] ought to be expelled from a definition. If with Campanella he defines "fever" as "the war instigated against disease by the powerful force of the spirit" or as "the spontaneous extraordinary agitation and inflammation of the spirit for giving battle to the irritant cause of the sickness," it is evident that the philosopher has provided an example of a nonproper definition, so that by it we can see more deeply into the nature of such definitions.[26] In place of a definition of "nonproper definitions" in general he has offered an individual case, and in place of a general concept of nonproper locutions he has offered representations of war, agitation of spirit, and inflammation, and so on, concepts in which more has been determined than that they are merely arrived at through a non-proper term, which, moreover, is merely added to this concept for expressing and manifesting it. That person will find our definition [of "example"] productive who attempts to solve the problem of how a teacher furnishes an example for showing the way to others, or who has meditated on the profound words of the pious Spener where he says, "Mathematics, through the certainty and safety of its demonstrations, provides an example for all sciences, which we emulate as far as we can." Cf. § 107.[27]

§ 22. Examples confusedly represented are representations that are extensively clearer than those for whose clarification they are offered, § 21; hence they are more poetic, § 18; and among them individual examples are, of course, the best, § 19.

The illustrious Leibniz sees this in that excellent book in which he undertakes to justify the ways of God, where he says, "The chief object of history, as well as of poetry, should be to teach prudence and virtue through examples."[28] When we look for an example of an example, we are confronted, rather like Tantalus, with such swimming abundance that we scarcely know which draught[29] to take. Let

us race off to the sea of the unhappy Ovid: the less determined representation—

*Often when one god oppresses, another god brings
help*[30]—

has scarcely escaped from his mouth, which drips with
salty streams of tears and sea water, when, behold! the
poet suddenly justifies himself, to the extent of six verses,
with a gathering flood of examples:

Vulcan stood against Troy, for Troy Apollo . . . , etc.[31]

§ 23. Concept A, which, independent of the characteristic
traits of concept B, is represented along with concept B, is said
to **adhere** to it. That concept to which another adheres is
called a **complex concept,** as opposed to a **simple concept**
to which no other adheres. Since a complex concept represents more than a simple one, confused complex concepts are
extensively clearer, § 16, and hence more poetic than simple
concepts, § 17.

§ 24. By **sense representations** we mean representations of
present changes in that which is to be represented, and these
are sensate, § 3, and thus far poetic, § 12.

§ 25. Since affects are rather marked degrees of pleasure or
pain, their sense representations are given in the representing
of something to oneself confusedly as good or bad.[32] Therefore, they determine poetic representations, § 24; and therefore, to arouse affects is poetic, § 11.

§ 26. The same can be demonstrated by this reasoning also:
we represent more in those things which we represent as good
or bad for us than if we do not so represent them; therefore,
representations of things which are confusedly exhibited as
good or bad for us are extensively clearer than if they were
not so displayed, § 16. Hence they are also more poetic, § 17.
Now such representations are rousings of the affects; therefore, to arouse affects is poetic, § 11.

§ 27. Stronger impressions are clearer impressions, thus more poetic than feeble and less clear impressions, § 17. Stronger impressions attend an affect more, rather than less, powerful, § 25. Therefore, it is highly poetic to excite the most powerful affects. This is evident from the following: that which we confusedly represent as the worst or as the best for us is represented more clearly, extensively, than if we had represented it as less good or less bad, § 16; and hence it is more poetic, § 17. Now the confused representation of a thing as very bad or very good for us determines the most powerful affects. Therefore, it is more poetic to excite more powerful, rather than less powerful, affects.

§ 28. Images are sensate representations, § 3, and so poetic, § 12.

When we call the reproduced representations of the senses "images," we of course follow philosophers in departing from the vague signification of the word, but not from the common usage of language or the rules of grammar: for who would deny that an image is what we have imagined? The faculty of imagining is already described in the lexicon of Suidas as "that which takes from perception the impressions of the things perceived and transforms them within itself."[33] What, then, are images if they are not newly made (reproduced) impressions (representations) received from sense? This is what is intended here under the concept of things sensed.

§ 29. Images are less clear than sense impressions, therefore, less poetic, § 17. Therefore, since aroused affects determine sense impressions, a poem which arouses affects is more perfect than one which is full of dead imagery, § 8, § 9, and it is more poetic to arouse affects than to produce other images. *It is not enough for poems to be beautiful: they must also be charming and lead the mind of the listener where they please.*[34]

Certainly a neat characteristic by which we can separate Homer from

Jackdaw poets and magpie poetesses,[35]

and from all those who, beginning with much promise,

Tack on a purple patch or two, to make a splurge.[36]

So Horace does not wholly condemn images. Let us see just which images these may be of whose cautious employment the poet, our touchstone, speaks.

So we are regaled with Diana's grove and altar (images 1 and 2), *or the river Rhine* (image 3), *or a rainbow* (image 4), *but this was not the place for them.*[37]

According to § 22, when the poet performs, we develop a more universal notion from these specific instances and sharp determinations, as it were from examples. Certainly no other notion will be found under which these things can be classified except that of imaged concepts. Not every place is suitable for an image; the reason is supplied by the foregoing proposition. If I may agree with Horace, the humblest craftsman who "depicts claws and imitates soft hair in bronze"[38] (aptly representing certain images in verse)

Fails in the consummation of the work because he does not know how to grasp the whole figure. Now if I cared to indulge in composition, I should no more want to be like that than to live with a crooked nose while admired for my dark hair and eyes.[39]

§ 30. When a partial image has been represented, the image of the object recurs as a whole and so far constitutes a complex concept of it, which, if it is confused, will be more poetic than if it is simple, § 23.[40] Therefore, to represent the whole with a partial image, and that extensively more clear, is poetic, § 17.

§ 31. That which, in respect to place and time, is coexistent with a partial image belongs with it to the same whole. There-

fore, to represent extensively clear images along with something to be partially represented is poetic, § 30.

The descriptions that poets use most are those of time, for
example, of night, of noon, and of evening in Virgil.⁴¹ The
four seasons of the year are depicted by Seneca in one passage;⁴² descriptions of dawn, of autumn, winter, springtime,
and so on, are also found in Virgil;⁴³ and to rival these, any
bad poet⁴⁴ you please can produce other specimens. Regarding these, however, the scholium to § 28 is especially to be
noted.⁴⁵

§ 32. That coexistent things are to be represented at the same
time, when they are represented in respect to place and time,
and so on, can be demonstrated as follows: it is poetic to represent as much as possible things that are very completely
determined, § 18; determinations of place and time are nu-
merical, or at least specific; therefore, they most completely
determine a thing. Therefore, to represent everything, and so
to determine images by disclosing things which coexist in
place and time, is poetic.

§ 33. When an image of a certain species or genus has been
represented, other images of the same species or genus will
recur. If such images are represented at the same time with
the genus or species, then, in part, the resultant concept may
be more complex and confused, and hence more poetic, § 23,
and in part, the genus or species may be more determined;
hence it is represented more poetically, § 20, § 19.

§ 34. If, with an image to be represented, a species or genus
which it has in common with other images is confusedly represented at the same time, it may be rendered extensively
more clear than if this has not been done, § 16; hence it is
poetic to represent a genus or species that the image to be
represented has in common with other images, § 17.

§ 35. If such images, which belong to the same genus or the same species to be represented together with a certain image, are represented at the same time, the genus will be represented more poetically than if this had been done in a different way, § 33. Now it is poetic to represent the genus or species with the image to be represented, § 34. Therefore, it is highly poetic to represent also, together with the image to be represented, the images belonging to the same genus or the same species.

§ 36. By **resemblances** we shall indicate the means by which a superior concept combines like with like. Therefore, resemblances pertain to the same species or the same genus. Therefore, it is highly poetic to represent resemblances along with an image to be represented, § 35.

> This is the reason why resemblances are exacted with such noisy insistence by those who teach budding oracles to sing under a master's rod. That there is a very smooth way of slipping into resemblances is evident from Virgil's example of Dido entering the temple of Juno. In this passage the poet causes a woman [Dido], conspicuously dressed in the highest fashion, to stand out from her companions.[46] All these traits, taken together, constitute a species, and Diana also belongs under it, but note, Diana has been a resemblance [not an example], for a resemblance is not an example when it is drawn from a person, § 17.[47]

§ 37. Representations of dreams are images, therefore poetic, § 28.

> We encounter these in Virgil, Ovid, Tibullus; but in what critics of pure poetry? And they are by no means to be rejected as such, even if our bile is stirred up by poets,
>
> *Whom frantic meanderings or lunacy strikes,*[48]
>
> so that they can know nothing but how to invent interpretations of dreams whenever Gaius weds his Gaia, or I don't

know what obscure light gutters in some microcosm or other.

§ 38. The more clearly images are represented, the more they will be similar to sense impressions, so that they are often equivalent to rather weak sensations. Now to represent images as clearly as possible is poetic, § 17. Therefore, it is poetic to make them very similar to sensations.

§ 39. It is the function of a picture to represent a composite, and that is poetic, § 24; the representation of a picture is very similar to the sense idea to be depicted, and this is poetic, § 38. Therefore, a poem and a picture are similar, § 30.

   Poetry is like a picture.[49]

For in this place the necessities of exegesis require one to concede that the grouping of poetry, meaning by this the poem, with painting, is to be understood in terms not of the art involved but of the effect achieved. Nor for this reason is there to be any argument about the genuine notion of poetry, correctly settled and established in § 9, for in such confusion of practically synonymous terms both our poet and others

   Have always had an equal right to hazard what they please.[50]

§ 40. Since a picture represents an image only on a surface, it is not for the picture to represent every aspect, or any motion at all; yet it is poetic to do so, because when these things are also represented, then more things are represented in the object than when they are not, and hence the representing is extensively clearer, § 16. Therefore, in poetic images more things tend toward unity than in pictures. Hence a poem is more perfect than a picture.

§ 41. Although images by way of words and discourse are clearer than those of visible things, nevertheless we are not trying to affirm a prerogative of a poem over a picture, since the *intensive* clarity which, through words, is granted to symbolic cognition beyond the intuitive, contributes nothing to *extensive* clarity, the only clarity that is poetic, § 17, § 14.

This is true both by experience and as a consequence of § 29.

Less vividly is the mind stirred by what finds entrance through the ear, than by what can be seen through one's own trusty eyes—what one can see for oneself.[51]

§ 42. A confused recognition of a representation is that of a sensate memory, and hence sensate, § 3, and poetic, § 12.

§ 43. By **wonder** we mean an intuition of many things in a representation, such things as are not found together in many series of our perceptions.

We agree with Descartes, who regards wonder as "a sudden seizure of the soul, in that it is lifted into a rapt consideration of objects which seem to it rare and extraordinary,"[52] with the reservation that, after rejecting from his definition whatever seems superfluous, we may adapt it to our chain of demonstration. While some think it unwise to suppose that the wonderful is merely the unusual, ignorance apart, we shall not reformulate the rule, but merely remark that in the extraordinary we sense, rather than implicitly assert, a relation to the inconceivable. We have tried, nevertheless, to indicate clearly the double source of wonder.

§ 44. Since intuitive cognition can be confused, it can also be wonder, § 43; hence, the representation of the wonderful is poetic, § 13.

§ 45. We generally pay marked attention to those things which have anything of the wonderful in them. Those things to which we pay such attention, if they are confusedly represented, are extensively clearer than those to which we do not, § 16. Therefore, representations which have anything of the wonderful in them are more poetic than those which do not.

Hence Horace:

> Silence now! Songs never before heard I, priest of the muses, sing to maids and boys.[53]

And perhaps the same things are suggested, if we separate the thought from the allegory in Ode 20, book II, where he begins,

> I shall be lifted on a wing which though untried is far from feeble.[54]

It may be objected that this concerns not the content but the form of the lyric, little cultivated by the Romans before Horace. Even so, this does not exclude content; and even if content were excluded, Horace would still excite, through his wonderful form, poetic representations, according to our proposition. And since in the very beginning of the poem he is eager for glory, as he declares openly, he has done well to say in praise of the poet, "untried," "never heard before," the one thing we wanted to point out.

§ 46. Where there is wonder, there also are present many things which are not recognized confusedly, § 43; therefore, they are less poetically represented, § 42.

Where there is confused recognition, there, it can be established a posteriori, wonder ceases. Suppose we observe someone in a state of wonder at something, for example, an artfully constructed implement of war. If we want to check his wonder, we can ask him whether he has not seen the same thing even more artfully constructed at Berlin or Dresden. If he remembers it, his wonder decreases.

§ 47. The representation of wonder is poetic, § 45; in another respect it is not, § 46; hence a conflict of rules and a necessary exception.

§ 48. If, therefore, wonders are to be represented, there ought still to be something that can be confusedly recognized in the representation of them, § 45; that is, to mingle skillfully the familiar with the unfamiliar in the wonderful itself is in the highest degree poetic, § 47.[55]

§ 49. Since miracles are individual actions, their representations are highly poetic, § 19; but since they occur most rarely in the realm of nature, or at least are rarely perceived there as such, they are indeed quite wonderful, § 43; hence familiar and very easily recognizable things must be introduced with them, § 48.

> *Let no god intervene unless a tangle occurs worthy of such a deliverer.*[56]

From the notion of a poem which we observe to have been established in § 9 comes that freedom to narrate the miraculous which is confirmed by numberless examples of the best poets. But if a poem should set itself the single goal of imitating nature, this freedom would degenerate into license. Nature certainly has nothing to do with miracles.

§ 50. Confused representations derived from elements separated and combined in the imagination are images and therefore poetic, § 23.

§ 51. The objects of such representations are either possible or impossible in the real world. Let the latter be called **fictions** and the former **true fictions.**

§ 52. Objects [denoted by] fictions are impossible in either of two ways, in the real world or in all possible worlds. Those which are absolutely impossible we shall call **utopian.** The others we shall term **heterocosmic.** Therefore, no representation of the utopian group can be formed; hence, none is confused, and none poetic.

§ 53. Only true and heterocosmic fictions are poetic, § 50, § 52.[57]

§ 54. By **descriptions** we mean enumerations of whatever parts there are in that which is represented. Therefore, if that which is confusedly represented is described, more parts are represented in it than if it is not described. But if it is what we shall call **confusedly described**, that is, if the confused representations of the parts are fully supplied in the describing, then it becomes extensively clearer. And this is true also: the more the parts that are confusedly represented, the clearer the description is, § 16. Therefore, confused descriptions and those most of all in which many parts are represented are in the highest degree poetic.

§ 55. Confused descriptions of sense impressions, images, and fictions, true and heterocosmic, are highly poetic, § 54.
Now we can ease a scruple which may trouble some heads. A description, by definition, is the distinguishing in A of B, C, D. So far as this is done, A is distinctly represented. Now, since this is contrary to our conception of a poem as set forth in § 9 and in § 14, which derives from § 9, it would be possible to deduce the absurdity that descriptions ought to be eliminated from a poem. We answer that B, C, D, and so on, are sensate representations, if we suppose them confused, § 3. Therefore, a description puts B, C, D, that is, several sensate representations, in place of a single sensate A. Hence if A should become distinct (but this would be rare), the poem, nevertheless, after description had been employed, would become more perfect than before, § 8.

§56. Since in the case of heterocosmic fictions many things can be presumed to enter the stream of thought of many listeners or readers—things which are not sense impressions or images or fictions or true fictions—they can be presumed wonderful, § 43. Therefore, in this case, much confused recognition, if it occurs, represents in the most poetic way a mingling of the familiar with the unfamiliar, § 48.

Hence Horace, "I shall look for my poetic fictions in familiar things,"[58] and when he would direct the poet, and teach him,

> *Where the poet draws his stores, what sustains and molds him, what befits him, what does not, where the right course leads him and where the wrong,*[59]

he bids the poet "follow the tradition and bring back Achilles,"[60] that is, to proceed according to § 17.[61] He tells us that the heroic subjects of the myths are the most familiar. Medea, Io, Ino, Ixion, Orestes are examples of the same concept of what constitutes the most tragic characters in the theater. Further on in the sequel Horace expressly states:

> *It would be better for you to spin out a tale of Ilium into acts than to be the first to offer a theme unknown, unsung.*[62]

We know that the poet is speaking of comedy, and the banquet of Thyestes [the drama], but since the principle determining the rule is, as already demonstrated, universal, the rule is also universal. The tale of Troy is another example of a well-known heterocosmic fiction. "To create a new character" he calls presumption.[63]

§ 57. Fictions in which there is much that is mutually inconsistent are utopian, not heterocosmic, § 52; hence there is nothing self-contradictory in poetic fictions, § 53.

> *Invent only what is self-consistent,*[64]

so that it can also be said as it is said of Homer,

> *So skillfully does he invent, so cleverly blend fact and fiction, that the middle is not discordant with the beginning, nor the end with the middle. The play must not require you to believe whatever it pleases, nor, when the Ogress has dined on the boy, draw him living and breathing from her gullet. Whatever things of this sort you expose me to, I discredit and abhor. Our most respected citizens drive from the stage any play that has no moral value.*[65]

§ 58. If any philosophical or universal theme whatever is to be represented poetically, it is wise to determine it as much as possible, § 18, by the introduction of examples, § 22, definite as to place and time, § 28,[66] and by description enumerating as many other details as possible, § 49.[67] If experience does not suffice, true fictions are available; if, indeed, the historical part is not rich enough, heterocosmic fictions are likely to be necessary, § 44, § 47.[68] Therefore, fictions both true and heterocosmic are, on condition, necessary in a poem.

We think nobody who considers the matter at all can be ignorant of certain aspects of the quarrel which the rhetoricians prosecute against the poets over whether or not fiction belongs to the essential nature of a poem. So we have not resolved the issue by a reluctant concession to either party, but rather have determined definite instances in which the poet is forced to have recourse to fiction. Experience teaches that fictions are not only admissible, but often even unavoidable. Whatever our portion in the City of God, we must render in verses that which promotes virtue and religion. It may be that poets have done just this throughout the changing fortunes of the past. (See the dissertation defended by Joh. Andr. Schmid at Helmstadt, *De modo propagandi religionem per carmina*).[69] Surely whatever tends, no matter how imperfectly, to restore the true perfection of the human race will be universal, and for the most part the words of a poet very often have to be made up from universal and less-determined notions. Horace long ago stated,

> *The Socratic writings will provide you with all the material you need.*[70]

Therefore, our first assumption is possible; the possibility of the second will be evident if one considers that the poet often writes for readers unknown to him at least, and so can hardly judge what will suggest things they have experienced. If he proposes images, not fictions, which the auditors or readers have not experienced, these are true fictions for them, § 44.[71] Very recent history, which is highly determined, ought to be familiar, but it is largely useless for the poet because it exposes him to the twin dangers of adulation and ridicule, or at least to a prominence which is difficult or indeed impossible to avoid. More remote history is never so determinately known as the pen of the poet requires—as already demonstrated. What is narrated, therefore, has to be more fully determined. Determinations have to be added to the poem about those things concerning which history is silent. They can be discerned only by taking note of whatever must be presupposed for their literal truth. But since this does not fall within the limits of comprehension, they must be guessed at from very little and often insufficient evidence. In this respect the truth of poetic inventions is decidedly improbable; that is, their nonexistence and their status among the heterocosmic fictions are probable.

§ 59. Since we may readily comprehend that the probable happens more often than the improbable, a poem which treats of probable events represents things more poetically than a poem which treats of improbable events, § 56.

As extensive as the realm of laudable fictions may be, it loses ground every day as the limits of sound reason are extended. One cannot say how many utopian fictions, contrary to § 47,[72] the wisest poets used to traffic in, such as adulterous gods and so on. Gradually this kind of thing has become ridiculous, until nowadays we must avoid not only contradictions in the poem but also any deficiency of reason or any effect contrived contrary to reason, as our poet so often warns:

> *If you want curtain calls or even most people to remain in their seats until the curtain line: "Now you may applaud!" you must observe the customs of each age.*[73]

Fidelity to custom determines whether an action or speech is treated thus and not otherwise. Suppose the contrary occurs:

Everybody, even commoners, will burst out laughing. The gentry will hardly receive with favor or reward with a crown everything that the buyers of roasted beans and chestnuts approve.[74]

Do you want the reason? Consult the proposition above. We do not deny that it is truly said, "There's many a slip 'twixt the cup and the lip,"[75] nor do we forbid the appearance of such things in a poem. We are inquiring here only concerning what is particularly poetic. Every occasion of the unexpected has its reason, until then unknown. Therefore, a representation of such an event contains the wonderful, § 43, and hence the poetic, § 44, § 45. If afterward, in the course of the narrative, the ground of the event is revealed, then the familiar is mingled with the unfamiliar, and the representation of such an event is more poetic than before, § 48.

§ 60. By **prevision** we mean the representation of the future; when expressed in words prevision is called **prediction**. If the prevision does not come from insight into the connection of the future with the conditions determining it, it is **presentiment**; and when presentiment is expressed in words, it is called **prophecy**.

§ 61. Future events are going to exist. Therefore, they are to be determined in every respect. Therefore, representations of them, that is, previsions, § 60, are particulars, hence highly poetic, § 19.

§ 62. If the connection of the thing to be previsioned with the conditions determining it were to be so indicated that it could be distinctly comprehended by the listener or reader, that

future would be demonstrated. Therefore, we should be drawing *distinct* conclusions, which is scarcely poetic, § 14. Therefore, poetic previsions are only presentiments, and poetic pre-
dictions only prophecies, § 60. Therefore, prophecy is poetic,
§ 61.

§63. If the future is not known in a natural or a supernatural
way, or is not known so determinately as is suitable for a
poem, then for the prophetic fictions the same conditional
necessity obtains which in § 58 was demonstrated especially
for the narration of things past.

§ 64. In prophetic fictions nothing ought to be self-contradictory, § 54, and probabilities are to be preferred to improb-
abilities, § 60.

> Prophecies become the poet beautifully. This is the reason
> why even in the Holy Scripture a good many prophets favor
> poetry. Yet it is dangerous to make predictions of things
> whose future state is unknown, and a prophecy belied by
> the event is sadly ridiculed. What should the poet do here?
> The cleverest of them prophesy in the name of others about
> things which have already come to pass, as if the prediction
> had anticipated the event. What does Helenus in Virgil not
> sing to Aeneas? Or Anchises in the Elysian Fields? Or the
> Cumean Sibyl? Or Vulcan about the shield?[76] Horace has
> Nereus predict the outcome of the Trojan War, since he
> knew he could invent prophecies which the outcome had
> already confirmed.[77] What Horace does is very often and
> very adroitly applied to the sacred history of Christianity
> by Sarbiewski, the foremost of recent lyric poets.[78] He
> beautifully depicts Noah looking out from the Ark and
> prophesying that one day he will be accorded divine honor
> and the like, which we now know without the spirit of
> prophecy. Likewise, pious fraud would have posterity be-
> lieve that it had "read the book of the Sibyl."[79]

§ 65. The interconnection of poetic representations must contribute to sensate cognition, § 7, § 9. Therefore, it must be poetic, § 11.

Such is the power of order and connection.[80]

§ 66. By **theme** we mean that whose representation contains the sufficient reason of other representations supplied in the discourse, but which does not have its own sufficient reason in them.

§ 67. If there are many themes, there can be no connection. Suppose that A is a theme, and B also; if they are connected, then either the sufficient reason of A is in B, or of B in A. Therefore, either A or B is not the theme, § 66. Interconnection is itself quite poetic, § 65; therefore, a poem having a single theme is more perfect than one which has several, § 8, § 11.

Thus we understand what Horace says,

Let the work (in the final representation) *be anything you wish, provided it is at least simple and uniform.*[81]

§ 68. It is poetic for sense impressions and images of a poem, which are not themselves themes, to be determined through the theme, for if they are not determined through it, they are not connected with it, and it is the interconnection that is poetic, § 65.

Now we have set limits and put a curb to the fantasy and unbridled license of the wits, which might shamefully abuse the preceding propositions, where we not only admitted images and fictions into a poem but assumed their perfection. Now we are in a position to see that representations may be altogether good independently of each other, but that in the coördination of them every sense idea, every fiction, every fantasy must be excluded

Which does not conform to the design (theme) *and blend into the plot.*[82]

We observed a little while ago that the poet is like a maker or a creator. So the poem ought to be like a world. Hence by analogy whatever is evident to the philosophers concerning the real world, the same ought to be thought of a poem.

§ 69. If poetic representations which are not themselves themes are determined through the theme, they will be connected with it. Therefore, they will be connected among themselves. Therefore, they follow each other in order, like causes and effects. Therefore, the degree of similarity observable in the succession of representations is the degree of order in the poem. Now it is poetic for poetic representations which are not themselves themes to be connected with the theme, § 69. [*Read:* § 68.] Therefore, order is poetic.

§ 70. Since order in a succession of representations is called **method**, method is poetic, § 69. And, with Horace, when he attributes a lucid order to poets, let us call that poetic method **lucid.**[83]

§ 71. The general rule of the lucid method is this: poetic representations are to follow each other in such a way that the theme is progessively represented in an extensively clearer way. Since the theme is to be set forth in a sensate manner, § 9, its extensive clarity is maintained, § 17. Now if the earlier representations represent more clearly than those that follow, the latter do not accord with what is to be poetically represented. But they ought to accord, § 68. Therefore, the later representations ought to set forth the theme more clearly than the earlier.

The ancients seem justly to have laughed at those cyclic poets who neglect this rule of method at the beginning of their poems, and as soon as they seize a pen,

Great mountains labor [and a silly mouse is born].[84]

Who does not condemn the "vast open jaws belching some

highflown verse"[85] of a poet who vents his Pegasean enthusiasm—after he has barely dipped himself in the Hippocrene font. At that very gate, moreover,

He casts up bombast and words a yard and a half long.[86]

We do not want to belabor again Lucan, Statius, and others whom many have abused for this fault. It seems preferable first to give the reason why these badly begun poems are begun as they are, then to extend the rule which they have transgressed to the whole range of poetry. Everywhere one ought to observe that practice which Horace judged so laudable in Homer:

How much better is he who makes no futile efforts. He strives to produce not smoke from flame, but after smoke the light, that he may disclose striking and wonderful tales—Antiphates and Scylla, Cyclops and Charybdis.[87]

Let us pare away the figurative language from the actual significance, and it will be obvious that the poet here agrees with the rule set forth in our proposition, even though he is concerned only with the opening of the poem. The other analogy to this rule is given in the rule of order by which things in the world follow one another for disclosing the glory of the Creator, the ultimate and highest theme of some immense poem, if one may so speak.

§ 72. Since, according to § 71,[88] certain of the coördinate ideas can cohere as premises with conclusions, certain as like with like and related with related, certain through the law of sensation and imagination, therefore there is available for lucid presentations the method of reason, the method of wit, and the method of the historians,[89] respectively.

§ 73. If the rules of method either of memory or of wit contradict poetic rules, for example § 71, yet other rules concur with them, then it is poetic to go over from one method to another, § 11.

We may so interpret Horace, when, though hesitantly, he lays down rules for order:

> *This, unless I am very wrong, will be the excellence and charm of order: let the poet say right now what must be said right now, and reserve and defer, for the present, a great deal else.*[90]

The things that "must be said" are those required by the method of wit or memory or reason—whichever was employed in what has gone before. Certain things the poet "says now," since there is order and method in the poem. Besides these methods or methods made up from them, scarcely any others can be conceived of. Certainly, then, the various parts of the poem must be combined by means of one or another of them. The poet "reserves for the present" because what follows from another order of thought is more suitable to the perfection of the poem and to that extent more poetic. We may concede that Horace had no *distinct* conceptions either of lucid method or any other, but there ought to be no doubt here about the true sense, provided that our conceptions represent the poet's, albeit perhaps more distinctly. See Wolff, *Logica*, § 929.[91]

§ 74. By **intrinsically or absolutely brief discourse** we mean that which has nothing in it that could be left out without loss of a degree of perfection. Such brevity, since it is proper to every discourse, is also proper to a poem, § 9.

And yet

> *It is true that little words have often marred or made men's fortunes.*[92]

We imagine that Horace has the same notion of brevity in mind when he says

> *Whenever you give instruction be brief.*

He adds at once,

Every word in excess seeps out of a mind already full,[93]
where it is quite evident that he opposes brevity to excess.
This definition of brevity also enables us to understand how
it can be that someone,
   While he tries to be brief, becomes only obscure,[94]
for since such a one is unwilling to be redundant by even
one tiny word, he so stuffs the speech with thoughts that
one thing cannot be distinguished from another; this produces obscurity. Extrinsic or relative brevity is not necessary
for every discourse or every poem. Even if it is proper to
particular sorts, for example, epigrams, it must be derived
from their constitution and specific determination—a matter with which I do not now wish to be concerned.

§ 75. Since nonpoetic and less-connected representations can
be left out of the poem without loss of a degree of poetic perfection, it is likewise poetic to leave them out, § 74, § 11.
   The same advice is given poetically by Horace in the example of Homer, see § 22,[95] when he praises in him that
   He abandons that which he fears he cannot make glow
   (make extensively more clear) *with his touch.*[96]
In the *Metamorphoses* of Ovid we can see how the poet
wades right through many tales with a dry foot, according
them scarcely three words, not without bawling and squall-
ing on the part of small boys who demand double helpings
of old wives' tales.

§ 76. It is advisable to omit certain elements from a poem, § 75.
If one were to try to present every interconnection of a historical theme, he might wonder if he should not include a
substantial part of the world, not to say all the history of the
ages: it is poetic to omit certain details and more remote
connections.
   What else does Homer do?—Homer, who, on the authority
of Horace, is the poet *par excellence,* § 22?[97]

*He always hurries to the issue and rushes the listener into
the midst of things, just as if they were already well
known.*[98]

"Midst" is used here as opposed to the twin egg (of Leda)
in the matter of the Trojan War.[99] This is relevant, but
rather remotely, to the other events, so that it would be
available for somebody not particularly concerned about
brevity to tell about it. What Horace says of Homer, someone who reflects on the opening of the *Aeneid* could say of
Virgil:

*Scarcely out of sight of Sicily, the joyful band set sail on
the deep,* etc.[100]

The same thing turns up in many comic poets. If you except
the prologue, their main characters begin their plotting
right off, as if the whole business were obvious, and this, because of § 65, is entirely appropriate.

§ 77. Since words belong among the parts of a poem, § 10,
they should be poetic, § 11, § 9.

§ 78. The aspects of words are: (1) articulate sounds, (2)
meaning. The more each is poetic, the more perfect the poem
is, § 7.

§ 79. Nonproper meaning lies in the nonproper word. Nonproper terms, since most of them are appropriate to sensate
representations, are poetic figures, because (1) the representation which approaches a thing through a figure is sensate,
hence poetic, § 10, § 11; and (2) these terms supply complex
confused representations in abundance, § 23.

§ 80. If the representation to be communicated in a poem does
not happen to be sensate and yet what is appropriate to a sensate representation is brought forth through a nonproper
term, there will emerge a representation at once complex and

confused, because a simple sensate representation is not united with anything else. Therefore, it is poetic to communicate non-sensate representations by means of nonproper terms.

As soon as we attempt to express tenderness, for example, there hovers before our minds either a distinct or a nonproper notion. The former is not poetic, § 14. The latter is aptly employed by Sarbiewski:

> *The brow is milder to behold, and the heavens at noon shine with a cloudless face. And he who protects all things is clear of the encircling cloud of wrath, lovelier than the first star of night—his face made beautiful in a rose-red rainbow.*[101]

§ 81. If whatever is to be communicated happens to be less poetic than the literal meaning of a nonproper term, then it is poetic that the nonproper term be preferred over the proper term, § 79.[102]

§ 82. Since clear representations are more poetic than obscure ones, § 13, it is poetic in figurative usages to avoid obscurity and to observe such limits in the number of them as are requisite for clarity.

§ 83. Metaphors are nonproper terms, hence poetic, § 79; likewise, they are highly poetic, § 36. Therefore, they are rightly more abundant than the other figures.

§ 84. Synecdoches are nonproper terms, putting species for genus and individuals for species, and therefore poetic, § 79, moreover, highly poetic, § 19, § 20. Therefore they are rightly employed in greater abundance than the remaining figures.

For example, Tiphys for sailors, Palinurus for a helmsman, Suffenus for him who without rivals loves only himself and his possessions, Chremes for a miser, Marrucinus for an oaf, Nepos for a spendthrift, Mentor for an artisan, Codrus for an envious man, Irus for a pauper, etc.[103]

§ 85. Since by **allegory** we mean a series of connected metaphors, it contains individual poetic representations, § 79, and more interconnection than where unrelated metaphors flow together. Thus allegories are highly poetic, § 65, § 8.

§ 86. Epithets provide a complex representation of a substantive. Therefore epithets, when they are not distinct, are poetic, § 23.

§ 87. By **superfluous epithets** we mean epithets designating attributes whose representations are only slightly connected with the theme. Therefore, it is poetic to avoid superfluous epithets, § 75. By **tautologous epithets** we mean epithets designating the same attribute already specified in the concept of the substantive. These are contrary to brevity, § 74, and it is poetic to avoid them.

§ 88. Since epithets designate representations, they can be best thought of according to the rules supplied above concerning poetic representations in general.

§ 89. Proper names are names designating individuals. Since these are highly poetic, proper names are also poetic, § 19.

§ 90. Since a confused recognition of a representation is poetic, § 42, and since mere proper names of unknown force[104] do not prompt further cognitions, they do not so far arouse wonder, § 43. It is poetic to be wary of a profusion of unfamiliar proper names, § 13.[105]

§ 91. Words, in the respect that they are articulate sounds, belong among audible things; hence they elicit sense perceptions.

§ 92. A confused judgment about the perfection of sensations is called a **judgment of sense,** and is ascribed to the sense organ affected by the sensation.

This will allow us to express *le gout* of the French as applied solely to the senses. It is obvious that this French expression is to be applied to a judgment by the senses, simi-
larly the Hebrew טעם and ראה , the Latin *loquere ut te
videam,* and the Italian society *del buon gusto.* Though
some of these modes of speaking may apply also to locution
about distinct cognition, we do not wish now to enter upon
this subject. It is sufficient that it is not contrary to usage to
attribute a confused judgment to the senses and to speak of
judgment of the senses.[106]

§ 93. The judgment of the ear is either positive or negative,
§ 91; the positive judgment produces pleasure, the negative
displeasure; since a confused representation determines both,
§ 92, it is sensate, § 3, and poetic, § 12. It is poetic to excite
either displeasure or pleasure in the ear, § 11.

§ 94. The more that is marked as harmonious or discordant,
the more intense the pleasure or displeasure. Every judgment
of sense is confused, § 92. Therefore, if judgment A observes
more to be harmonious or discordant than judgment B, A
will be extensively clearer than B, § 16, hence more poetic,
§ 17. Therefore, it is supremely poetic to produce the highest
pleasure or displeasure in the ear.

§ 95. If the highest displeasure is produced in the ear, it will
distract the attention of the listener. Hence, either few or no
representations can be further communicated and the poem
fails altogether of its purpose, § 5. Therefore, it is poetic to
produce in the ear the highest pleasure, § 94.

§ 96. Since the poem, taken as a series of articulate sounds,
excites pleasure in the ear, § 92, § 91, there must also be a perfection in it, § 92, and indeed the highest perfection, § 94.

§ 97. From this we can easily deduce the necessary purity of
the poem, the elegance of arrangement, the ornateness of the

figures. But these things the poem has in common with imperfect sensate discourse. We may, then, easily pass them over so as not to wander too far from our purpose. There will, therefore, be nothing here about the character of a poem as a series of articulate sounds: why one should avoid a rushing together of vowels, an overabundance of elision, and heavy alliteration. All ready perfection in the qualities of articulate sounds can be called **sonority**, a term, if I mistake not, borrowed from the school of Priscian.

§ 98. By **quantity of a syllable** we mean that property which cannot be known apart from association with another syllable. Therefore, quantity cannot be known from the value of the letters.

It pleases certain Hebrew philologists to attribute a given quantity to the syllables from the equal temporal measure of the letters. This quantity is hardly to be confused with ours. Christian Ravius, in his *Hebrew Orthography,* says: "Length and shortness of the syllable are to be understood here entirely as orthographic, not as prosodic, matters, lest anyone should deceive or be deceived."[107] According to this orthography—it is far from our present purpose to supply a distinct conception of it,—Hebrew syllables are all said to be equal. According to our definition of poetic quantity, this could never be posited except very wrongly.

§ 99. If in speaking we allot to every syllable its quantity, we are said to **scan.**

§ 100. If the value of a syllable A in scanning equals the value of syllable B plus the value of syllable C, A is said to be "long," C and B "short."

Amongst the grammarians, the value of a letter is the unit of time necessary for pronouncing it. Now, since the matter concerns only syllables, by the "duration of a syllable" we shall understand, allowing necessary changes, the unit of time necessary for pronouncing the syllable. Thus, in scanning, as much time as the quantity of the syllable requires, so much will be its value. This cannot be known unless we assume some syllabic value as the unit. This is the "short" syllable. The double of this duration gives the "long." From this we may derive the corollary that, if we maintain the quantity necessary for scanning, we may substitute $B + C$ for A. Said and done. Let us apply this to the simple scheme of the iambic senarius which can be resolved thus:

$$\cup - | \cup - | \cup - | \cup - | \cup - | \cup -$$

That iambic verse may fall somewhat more slowly and with more weight on the ear, it has received the steady spondee into its own domain, obligingly and tolerantly, but not so much as to yield the second and fourth places in the friendly ranks.[108]

Add the sixth also, lest it become a scazon, but when this takes place it does not yield the fifth. Now we have

$$\left. \frac{\cup -}{- -} \right| \left. \frac{\cup -}{- -} \right| \left. \frac{\cup -}{- -} \right| \cup - \left| \frac{\cup -}{- -} \right| \cup - .$$

Gradually if there is a substitution of two shorts for one long, all kinds of license will come into effect. At first, equal feet allow $\cup\cup$ for the second long syllable, whence the tribrach. Then, in the odd feet, for the first long we get $\cup\cup$, whence the anapaest; for the second long $\cup\cup$, whence dactyls with the final syllable long, as with the first short we had the tribrach. "Anapaests and dactyls are never found in the even feet, for there we never have a spondee," as Hephaestion teaches in his treatise on meter.[109] Even the proceleusmatic is possible, $\cup\cup\cup\cup$, but usage opposes it. In the same way we could present the licenses of the trochaic type and explain why it is that in certain senarii, according to usage, an anapaest stands at the beginning, and so on with the rest of it. Such an approach contributes much also to rational instruction of the young and to the gentle molding of their impressionable minds to serious things.

§ 101. If long and short syllables are so mingled that pleasure of the ear ensues, there is **measure** in the speech.

I have deemed it sufficient to offer a real rather than a nominal definition of a thing whose very existence is often called into doubt. Experience will now be constituted the judge. Measure is a matter of taste, § 92. Who will argue about this? The experience of others, and chief among them Cicero, is enough for our part. Thus his judgment and that of the other grammarians is that measure is by no means to be sought only in the varied arrangement of syllabic tones, but instead in the length and brevity of syllables irrespective of tones. Their variety is not, of course, felt distinctly if they are not scanned, but it is observed confusedly by the mind and to this extent furnishes sufficient matter for the judgment of the ear. If measure depended entirely on the position and tone of syllables, how, I ask, could one condemn the periodic clausula *"Petrum videatur"* and praise *"esse videatur"*? They have the same tone, not the same poetic quantity. This is especially evident in Greek, for if you assume the accents to be indications of tone, your eyes will soon be opened when you examine the poets. No sort of order or weight is apparent in the arrangement of the syllabic tones, but much accuracy in the observation of quantities. See J. Carpovius, *Meditatio de linguae perfectione.*[110]

§ 102. Measure produces pleasure in the ear, § 101. Therefore it is poetic, § 95.

§ 103. The kind of measure that, through the ordering of all syllables of the discourse, promotes pleasure in the ear is called

meter. If measure determines pleasure through many syllables following one another without any definite order, it is called **rhythm.** Therefore, since more contributes to the pleasure of the ear in the case of meter than in that of rhythm, more pleasure ensues from the former than from the latter; and so meter is poetic, § 95.

§ 104. By **verse** we mean metric or bounded[111] discourse. Therefore, when discourse is verse it tends toward the perfection of a poem, § 103, § 11.

§ 105. Not every instance of verse is a poem. Verse is perfected by meter, § 104. Therefore, when there is meter in discourse, there is verse. Now there can be meter in a discourse in which there are no sensate representations, no lucid order, no purity, no elegance of arrangement, and so on; and there can even be verse from which these things are missing. But by the preceding propositions and § 9 there cannot be a poem. Therefore, some verses are not poems.

We rightly distinguish with great care between poets and versewrights. We are paying our respects to those little paper twists of cracklings and pepper[112] which are cooked up for us every day as verses, never as poems. Most of them would blush at such an august title, if paper could blush, or if the shamelessness of the parents did not corrupt the progeny.

§ 106. End rhyme, which is nowadays called "rhythm," contrary to correct usage, § 103, the play of letters in acrostics, the working out of configurations—for example, a cross, a pear, a cone, and so on,—and many other scabrous forms, either exhibit only surface perfections or are determined under special conditions for a certain group of people through auricular judgment. So also lyric, epic, dramatic forms, with their subdivisions, have their peculiarities. These, to be sure, ought to conform to the perfections of their type, but we cannot demonstrate that they do except by reference to predetermined definitions of whatever species they may happen to belong to. Moreover, there are modes of presentation, chant and affecting recitation or dramatic action, which, since they contributed wonderfully to the purpose of a poem, enjoyed extraordinary esteem amongst the ancients, as long as these modes were confined to their limits. If they overstep them, as they do now in our theater, they impede more than promote the enjoyment that ought to be derived from a poem. Such observations have often been made and need not be repeated here.

§ 107. Since meter produces sense impressions by § 103, § 102, and since these have the greatest extensive clarity, they are to that degree the most poetic, and more so than those less clear, § 17. Thus it is highly poetic to observe most carefully the laws of meter, § 29.

> "We must catch the lawful beat by ear or finger. The measures of Plautus are far too tolerantly endured, not to say stupidly praised,"[113] and although, especially in our age, *Not every critic discerns unmusical poems, and we grant undeserved indulgence to our Roman poets, am I therefore to run loose and write without restraint? Or am I to suppose that everyone will observe my errors?*[114]

§ 108. If a person is said to **imitate**, he imitates something in that he produces something else similar to it. Hence an effect similar to something else can be said to be an **imitation** of it, whether it is done intentionally or from some other cause.

§ 109. If a poem is regarded as an imitation of nature or of an action, its effects must be similar to those produced by nature, § 107.[115]

> *Alphesiboeus will imitate the dancing satyrs.*[116]

§ 110. Representations to be produced immediately from nature, that is, from the intrinsic principle of change in the universe and from actions dependent on this, can never be distinct and intelligible, since they are sensate, but they are extensively clear, § 24, § 16, and as such poetic, § 9, § 17. Therefore, nature (if we be allowed to speak of a substantialized phenomenon together with the actions dependent on it as if of the substance itself) and the poet create resemblances, § 26.[117] Hence, the poem is an imitation of nature and of the actions depending on it, § 108.

§ 111. If anyone should define "poem" as "bounded discourse" ("verse" by § 104), and as "an imitation of actions or of nature," he would have two basic concepts not determined in order one from the other. But both are determinable from our propositions, § 104, § 109. Therefore, to agree with this result seems to approach the essence of a poem in what is perhaps the proper way.

See the *Poetics* of Aristotle, the *De artis poeticae natura et constitutione* of Voss, and the *In arte critica poetica* of the celebrated Joh. Christ. Gottsched.[118]

§ 112. We call that **vivid** in which we are allowed to perceive many parts either simultaneously or in succession.

This definition may be compared to the usage of language. We call a picture painted in the most variegated color *"ein lebhaftes Gemälde."* We call a discourse offering all sorts of perceptions to occupy us, as much in the sound as in the meaning, *"einen lebhaften Vortrag,"* and intercourse in which all sorts of events follow one another and we are in no fear of falling asleep, *"einen lebhaften Umgang."*

§ 113. Someone might define "poem," with the estimable Arnold, in his essay *In dem Versuch einer Systematischen Einleitung zur Teutschen Poesie,*[119] as "a discourse which by

attention to tonal qualities (meter) represents a thing as vividly as possible and which with its whole power of comprehension insinuates itself into the soul of the reader so that it
can move him in a definite way." If one should do this, the
following characteristics of the poem would be established:
(1) meter, (2) representations as vivid as possible, (3) action
tending to move the soul of the reader. The first is demonstrated by our § 104; the second is extensively clear representations, by § 111,[120] § 16; the third follows from our § 25, § 26,
§ 27.

§ 114. The definition of "poetry" of the estimable Walch in
his *Philosophical Lexicon* is as follows: "a species of eloquence, in which, with the help of native talent (which by
itself does not make a poet) we clothe our primary thoughts
(themes) with various ingenious and graceful thoughts or
images or representations, whether this in free or bounded
discourse."[121] The definition seems too broad, and what he
calls "the language of affects" too narrow. But that which he
rightly attributes to poetry can likewise be determined from
our propositions.

§ 115. Philosophical poetics is by § 9 the science guiding sensate discourse to perfection; and since in speaking we have
those representations which we communicate, philosophical
poetics presupposes in the poet a lower cognitive faculty. It
would now be the task of logic in its broader sense to guide
this faculty in the sensate cognition of things, but he who
knows the state of our logic will not be unaware how unculti-
vated this field is. What then? If **logic** by its very definition
should be restricted to the rather narrow limits to which it is
as a matter of fact confined, would it not count as the science
of knowing things philosophically, that is, as the science for
the direction of the higher cognitive faculty in apprehending
the truth? Well, then. Philosophers might still find occasion,

not without ample reward, to inquire also into those devices
by which they might improve the lower faculties of knowing,
and sharpen them, and apply them more happily for the bene-
fit of the whole world. Since psychology affords sound principles, we have no doubt that there could be available a
science which might direct the lower cognitive faculty in
knowing things sensately.

§ 116. As our definition is at hand, a precise designation can
easily be devised. The Greek philosophers and the Church
fathers have already carefully distinguished between *things
perceived* [αἰσθητά] and *things known* [νοητά]. It is entirely
evident that they did not equate *things known* with things of
sense, since they honored with this name things also removed
from sense (therefore, images). Therefore, *things known* are
to be known by the superior faculty as the object of logic;
things perceived [are to be known by the inferior faculty,
as the object] of the science of perception, or **aesthetic.**[122]

§ 117. The philosopher presents his thought as he thinks it.
Hence there are no special rules, or only a few, that he must
observe in presenting it. He has no special interest in terms,
so far as they are articulate sounds, for as such they belong
among the *things perceived*. But he who presents sensate subject matter is expected to take much greater account of terms.
Hence that part of aesthetics which treats of such presentation is more extensive than the corresponding part of logic.
Now since presentation can be either of an unperfected or of
a perfected character, it will be the concern of general rhetoric
or of general poetics, respectively. **General rhetoric** may be
defined as the science which treats generally of unperfected
presentation of sensate representations, and **general poetics**
as the science which treats generally of the perfected presentation of sensate representations. The one is divided into sacred,
profane, judicial, demonstrative, deliberative forms, and so

on, the other into epic, dramatic, lyric forms, with their sundry analogous species. But philosophers may leave the division of these arts to rhetoricians, who implant historical and experimental knowledge of them in the minds of their students. The philosophers should be busy in general in drawing boundary lines and especially in defining accurate limits between poetry and ordinary eloquence. The difference is, to be sure, only a matter of degree; but in the relegation of things to one side or the other it requires, we think, no less capable a geometer than did the frontiers of the Phrygians and the Mysians.

THE END

Notes

[1] The author uses the plural to include his brother Nathanael, named on the title page as respondent for the dissertation.

[2] Meier, faithful disciple and biographer of Baumgarten, says that Martin Christgau had been obligated to Baumgarten's father and that in 1727 he became rector of the Berlin gymnasium. Georg Friedrich Meier, *Alexander Gottlieb Baumgartens Leben*, Halle, 1763, pp. 8–9. Cf. Croce's edition of the *Meditationes*, Naples, 1900, p. 3, note.

[3] This echoes Juvenal, *Satires*, II, 152.

[4] The phrase means discourse for external utterance as opposed to that restrained within. For Aristotle's definition of "proposition" see *De interpretatione*, 16b26.

[5] The missing premise would have to say that anything which designates connected representations permits connected representations to be apprehended from it.

[6] Cf. Aristotle, *Metaphysica*, 996b26 ff., *Analytica posteriora*, 75a38 ff.

[7] Cicero, *Tusculan Disputations*, V, vii, 18. The word "defined" (*definito*) is interpolated by Baumgarten.

[8] A reference to the famous prohibition attributed to Plato: "Let no one without geometry enter here!" (i.e., into the Academy).

[9] Cf. Christian Wolff, *Psychologia empirica*, § 580: "Appetitus sensitivus dicitur, qui oritur ex idea boni confusa." ("Sensate appetite is to be defined as that which arises from a confused idea of the good.")

[10] Julius Caesar Scaliger (1488–1558), *Poetices, libri VII*, 1561. Gerardus Ioannes Vossius (or Voss) (1577–1649), *De artis poeticae natura*, 1647.

[11] Nonius Marcellus and Aelius Donatus, grammarians of the fourth century A.D., and Aelius Festus Aphthonius of the third century A.D. Gaius Lucilius, satirist of the second century B.C. The grammarians are represented by extant works. The fragments of Lucilius are found chiefly in Nonius.

[12] Horace, *Ars poetica* (abbreviated henceforth as *A.P.*), 72.

[13] The word in question is *poesis*. The first reference to Cicero is to *Tusculan Disputations,* V, xxxix, 114: "Traditum est etiam Homerum caecum fuisse. At eius picturam, non poesim videmus." This may be translated: "There is a tradition also that Homer was blind. Yet what *we* see is his painting, not his poetry." As to the second reference, Baumgarten scolds Voss for what is an obvious slip of the pen, as there is no book VI. The passage referred to is a single line: "Nam Anacreontis quidem tota poesis est amatoria," IV, xxxiii, 71, the only mention, it would seem, of Anacreon in any book of the *Tusculan Disputations:* "And as to Anacreon, of course, all his poetry is love poetry."

[14] Persius, *Satires,* IV, 49–50. The interpretation is not so simple as Baumgarten seems to think. See note xx in John Conington's commentary and translation of Persius, edited by Nettleship (Clarendon Press, 1893, p. 83). Conington's translation of the passage reads thus: "If in your zeal for the main chance you flag the exchange with many a stripe, it will do you no good to have made your thirsty ears the receptacle of popular praise." This is a strange interpretation. Conington and Nettleship ignore Neronian history as a basis for interpretation of a very difficult passage.

[15] No source for the verses is given. Probably an invention of Baumgarten.

[16] Baumgarten refers here to Choerilus, a poet of the fourth century B.C., referred to as a worthless poet in *A.P.* 357–358.

[17] Homer, *Iliad,* II, 484 ff., the famous catalogue of the ships.

[18] Ovid., *Metamorphoses,* 3, 206–224.

[19] Horace, *Odes,* I, 1.

[20] Tibullus, III, 2, 23–25.

[21] Apparently an invented example.

[22] Virgil, *Eclogues,* I, 50.

[23] The reference is to the storm which Juno persuades Aeolus to send against the Trojans, who are sailing for Italy under Aeneas, *Aeneid,* I, 181–197.

[24] The line quoted is c. 64, 256. The following eight lines to which Baumgarten refers may be rendered: "Others were tossing about limbs torn from a mangled calf; others were girding themselves with writhing serpents; others were carrying dark mysteries in caskets—mysteries that the uninitiated crave in vain to know about. Still others were beating on timbrels with uplifted hands or raising thin tinkling sounds with rounded brass. Many were blowing raucous blasts on horns, and the outlandish pipes were shrill with dreadful din."

[25] See propositions 80 ff. for "nonproper terms." Cf. also Wolff, *Logica*, § 138 (definition of proper terms), § 146 (definition of non-proper terms).

[26] Tommaso Campanella (1568–1639), the celebrated author of the *City of the Sun*.

[27] Philipp Jakob Spener, Protestant theologian (1635–1705), often regarded as the father of Pietism. The passage quoted is *Consilia et iudicia theologica latina, opus postumum*, Frankfurt am Main, 1700, p. 214. The reference at the end to § 107 is in all likelihood a misprint for § 17 of the *Reflections*.

[28] Leibniz, *Essais de Théodicée*, II, § 148: "Le but principal de l'histoire, aussi bien que de la poésie, doit être d'enseigner la prudence et la vertu par des examples, et puis de montrer le vice d'une manière qui en donne de l'aversion, et qui porte ou serve à l'éviter."

[29] *Potissimum*, a pun on Tantalus' drink: cf. *affluentia* above, and the number of water figures that follow.

[30] Ovid, *Tristia*, I, 2, 4.

[31] The next verse of the *Tristia*, in quoting which Baumgarten, by an obvious *lapsus calami*, writes *Achilles* for *Apollo*.

[32] Wolff, *Psychologia*, § 605: "Affectus ex confusa boni et mali repraesentatione oriuntur." ("Affects arise from a confused representation of good and evil.")

[33] "Lexicon of Suidas": a lexicon dating from the tenth century A.D.

[34] Horace, *A.P.*, 99–100.

[35] Persius, Introduction to his *Satires*, line 13. The context is that, where there is enough money about, "you would be ready to believe that jackdaw poets and magpie poetesses are yielding the nectar of the Muses."

[36] Horace, *A.P.*, 14 f.

[37] These lines, 16–19, follow directly on the preceding, but Baumgarten omits 17:

> Et properantis aquae per amoenos ambitus agros.

[38] A paraphrase of *A.P.*, 32–33.

[39] The passage which directly follows, that is, *A.P.* 34–37. Our translation here, as often, follows our modern texts, not Baumgarten.

[40] Cf. Baumgarten, *Metaphysica*, § 561: "Lex imaginationis: percepta idea partiali recurrit eius totalis. Haec propositio etiam associatio idearum dicitur." This we may render: "The law of the imagination: an idea perceived of a part of a thing recurs as the whole of it. This proposition is also referred to as the association of ideas."

[41] A reference to the famous description of night in *Aeneid,* IV, 522-528 (when Dido planned her own death); of noon, *Eclogues,* II, which is set in the heat of midday, when even the lizards hide in the shade; and of evening, *Eclogues,* I, 82-83: "And now in the distance the smoke rises from the roofs of the village, and longer shadows fall from the high hills."

[42] It is typical of Seneca's rhetoric that he describes phenomena of nature such as the seasons. For an interesting passage involving the four seasons, cf. *Medea,* 752-769, where Medea describes how her magic often reversed the normal course of nature.

[43] *Georgics*—the whole poem is a sort of almanac of the seasons in the country and the hours of the day and night; II, 319-345, provides, for example, a well-known description of spring, when there is a spell of calm weather "between cold and heat" and "the green grass trusts itself to the spring sun."

[44] The word *adversaria* gives an untranslatable pun (-*vers*-).

[45] The scholium to § 29 is intended.

[46] *Aeneid,* I, 496 ff. Dido is likened to Diana, who is explicitly stated to be a goddess superior in a train of goddesses:

... gradiens deas supereminet omnes

(501)

(and as she walks, she towers above all the other goddesses).

[47] Perhaps § 19 is intended. The Latin for "resemblance" here is "*similia.*"

[48] Horace, *A.P.,* 454.

[49] Horace, *A.P.* 361 f.

[50] Horace, *A.P.* 10. See scholium to § 9 about the difficulty over "*poesis.*"

[51] Horace, *A.P.* 180-182.

[52] *Traité des passions de l'âme,* II, 70.

[53] *Odes,* III, 1, 2-4, the omitted first line ("I hate the vulgar throng and I keep my distance") being as well known as anything in Horace.

[54] *Odes,* II, 20, 1-2.

[55] § 45 is meant.

[56] Horace, *A.P.* 191-192. The *deus ex machina* device in drama.

[57] § 51 and § 52 yield § 53, not § 50 and § 52.

[58] *A.P.* 240.

[59] *A.P.* 307-308, reversed.

[60] *A.P.* 119–120.

[61] See also § 19.

[62] *A.P.* 129–130.

[63] *A.P.* 126. The word we translate as "presumption" is *audaciam,* but Horace does not use *audacia* in the present context.

[64] *A.P.* 119.

[65] These lines are a collection, grammatically independent, of several passages in A.P. They read as follows, corrected in several places:

> Atque ita mentitur, sic veris falsa remiscet,
> Primo ne medium, medio ne discrepet imum.
> $$(151–152)$$
> Nec quodcumque volet, poscat sibi fabula credi,
> Neu pransae Lamiae vivum puerum extrahat alvo.
> $$(339–340)$$
> Quodcumque ostendis mihi sic, incredulus odi.
> $$(188)$$
> Centuriae seniorum agitant expertia frugis.
> $$(341)$$

[66] § 32 is meant.

[67] This is obviously an error; § 54 will do.

[68] These references are also obviously incorrect: § 53 and § 56 fit best.

[69] That is, *Concerning the Way to Promote Religion Through Poetry;* Croce, *op. cit.,* p. 24, note, says this was published in 1710.

[70] *A.P.* 310.

[71] Another incorrect citation; § 51 is perhaps intended.

[72] § 57 is meant.

[73] *A.P.* 153–156.

[74] *A.P.* 113 and 249–250.

[75] *Anthologia graeca,* X, 32. Quoted by Aristotle, *Constitution of the Samians,* Aulus Gellius, XIII, 17, 1, or Valentin and Rose, fragment 571.

[76] The references to Virgil are as follows: *Aeneid,* III, 379 ff.; VI, 713 ff.; VI, 83 ff. For Vulcan see Homer, *Iliad,* XVIII, 464 ff.

[77] *Odes,* I, 15.

[78] Maciej Kazimierz Sarbiewski, seventeenth-century Polish Jesuit and poet, called the "Sarmatian Horace," which may explain Baumgarten's admiration for him (see scholium to § 80 for a brief sample of his verse).

[79] Juvenal, *Satires,* 8, 126.

[80] *A.P.* 242.

[81] *A.P.* 23.

[82] *A.P.* 196.

[83] Horace's words are "lucidus ordo," *A.P.* 41.

[84] *A.P.* 139.

[85] *A.P.* 457.

[86] *A.P.* 97.

[87] *A.P.* 140, 143–145.

[88] § 69 is meant.

[89] The "method of historians" is the "method of memory" of the following proposition.

[90] *A.P.* 42–44, the lines following immediately on the mention of "lucid order" (41).

[91] Wolff, *Logica,* § 929: "Quodsi autor cum quibusdam terminis conjungit notionem confusam, lector autem distinctam, et utraque eadem res repraesentatur; lector mentem autoris intelligit et melius explicat." This may be rendered: "If the writer joins a confused notion with certain terms, but the reader a distinct notion, and yet the same thing is represented in both cases, then the reader understands and makes more explicit the sense of the writer."

[92] Sophocles, *Electra,* 415–416.

[93] *A.P.* 335 and 337.

[94] *A.P.* 25–26.

[95] The scholium to § 57 touches on Horace's view of Homer. § 22 seems irrelevant.

[96] *A.P.* 149–150.

[97] See note 95 above.

[98] *A.P.* 148–149.

[99] Helen was hatched from an egg laid by Leda. Baumgarten is saying, in effect, that the poet need not begin at the remotest origins of a train of events, but like Homer may begin where it suits him.

[100] *Aeneid,* I, 34.

[101] For Sarbiewski see note 78 above.

[102] The notion behind this and the cited proposition, § 79, seems to be that poetic terms (nonproper terms), such as metaphors and other tropes, are proper to sensate representations.

[103] Tiphys is the pilot of the Argo; Palinurus, Aeneas' pilot; Suffenus, made notorious by Catullus (c. 22) as a poet who "so delights in him-

self, so admires himself" that nobody can endure him; Chremes, a small measure for a drink, sometimes used as a proper name for a miser; Marrucinus, one of the Marrucini, that is, residents in a country area some distance from Rome; Nepos, a spendthrift; Mentor, a celebrated artisan in raised metalwork; Codrus, a poet hostile to Virgil, *Eclogues,* 7, 26: Irus, a beggar in the house of Odysseus (see *Odyssey,* XVIII).

[104] Perhaps like some of the names in the preceding note!

[105] See also § 48.

[106] Baumgarten's point is that different languages have expressions which, derived from the sensations, apply to judgments of them, like the English "good taste." For explanation of the Hebrew and the Italian, see the edition of Baumgarten's *Aesthetica* published at Bari, 1936, p. 546. In that edition the following is suggested regarding the two Hebrew expressions: "The force of the first is 'he has tasted, has explored the flavor,' and by transference 'he has perceived in his soul'; that of the other 'to smell,' ... and by transference 'to smell out, to have a presentiment of.'" The Latin expression translates, "Speak so that I see you."

[107] Christian Ravius (1613–1677), publisher of grammars on Oriental languages.

[108] *A.P.* 255–258.

[109] This is *Enchiridion de metris et poemate Graeco et Latino,* by Hephaestion, a Greek scholar of the second century of our era. This treatise on meter is still extant; Baumgarten is quoting from a Latin translation.

[110] Jacob Carpovius, *Meditatio philosophico-critica de perfectione linguae, methodo scientifica adornata,* 1747.

[111] We translate ἔμμετρος as "bounded."

[112] After Martial, *Epigrams,* III, 2, 5.

[113] This is a rough version of *A.P.* 274, 271–273.

[114] *A.P.* 263–266.

[115] Proposition § 108 is clearly meant.

[116] Virgil, *Eclogues,* V, 73.

[117] A misprint for § 36.

[118] Aristotle, *Poetics,* 1; cf. note 11 above for Voss. Johann Christoph Gottsched (1700–1766) exercised major influence over the development of German style in the middle of the eighteenth century. The work cited is *Versuch einer Kritischen Dichtkunst,* first published at Leipzig, 1730.

[119] Daniel Heinrich Arnold; the book was apparently first published in Königsberg, 1732.

[120] This is a misprint for § 112.

[121] Johann Georg Walch, 1693–1775, famous editor of Luther's works in twenty-four volumes; the first edition of the *Philosophical Lexicon* was published at Leipzig in 1728. The parentheses are Baumgarten's.

[122] Plotinus, *Enneads,* IV, 8, 7. Διττῆς δὲ φύσεως ταύτης οὔσης, τῆς μὲν νοητῆς, τῆς δὲ αἰσθητῆς . . . ("This nature has two aspects, the one intelligible, the other sensible . . ."). The parallelism implied in Baumgarten's last sentence is made explicit in the translation.

Selected Bibliography

BAUMGARTEN, A. G.
Aesthetica, Part I, 1750, Part II, 1758, Frankfort on the Oder.
Aesthetica, iterum edita ad exemplar prioris editionis annorum MDCCL–LVIII spatio impressae, praepositae sunt *Meditationes philosophicae de nonnullis ad poema pertinentibus,* ab eodem auctore editae anno MDCCXXXV, Barii, Jos. Laterza et Filios, MCMXXXVI.
Meditationes philosophicae de nonnullis ad poema pertinentibus, Halle, 1735.
Meditationes philosophicae de nonnullis ad poema pertinentibus, ristampa dell'unica edizione del 1735, a cura di Benedetto Croce, Napoli, 1900.
Metaphysica, Halle, 1739.

BAEUMLER, ALFRED
Kants Kritik der Urteilskraft, Ihre Geschichte und Systematik, Bd. I: Das Irrationalitätsproblem in der Aesthetik und Logik des 18. Jahrhunderts bis zur Kritik der Urteilskraft, Halle (Saale), Max Niemeyer Verlag, 1923.

BERGMANN, ERNST
Die begründung der deutschen Aesthetik durch Alexander Gottlieb Baumgarten und Georg Friedrich Meier, mit einem Anhang: G. F. Meiers ungedruckte Briefe, Leipzig, 1911.

BOSANQUET, BERNARD
A History of Aesthetic, London, G. Allen & Unwin, 1892 et seq., pp. 182–187.

CROCE, BENEDETTO
Aesthetic as Science of Expression and General Linguistic, translated from the Italian by Douglas Ainslie, London, Macmillan, 1909 et seq., Part II: History of Aesthetic, pp. 212–219.

GILBERT, KATHARINE EVERETT, AND HELMUT KUHN
A History of Esthetics, revised and enlarged, Bloomington, Indiana University Press, 1953, pp. 289–295.

MEIER, GEORG FRIEDRICH
Alexander Gottlieb Baumgartens Leben, Halle, 1763.
Anfangsgründe aller Schönen Wissenschaften, Halle, 1748–1750.

MEYER, HANS GEORG
Leibniz und Baumgarten als Begründer der deutschen Aesthetik, Diss. Halle, 1874.

POPPE, BERNHARD
Alex. Gottl. Baumgarten, seine Stellung und Bedeutung in der Leibniz-Wolffischen Philosophie und seine Beziehung zu Kant, nebst Veröffentlichung einer bisher unbekannten Handschrift der Aesthetik Baumgartens, Diss. Münster, Leipzig, 1907.

RIEMANN, ALBERT
Die Aesthetik Alexander Gottlieb Baumgartens unter besonderer Berücksichtigung der *Meditationes de nonnullis ad poema pertinentibus,* nebst einer Uebersetzung dieser Schrift, Halle (Saale), Verlag von Max Niemeyer, 1928.

SCHMIDT, JOH.
Leibniz und Baumgarten, ein Beitrag zur Geschichte der deutschen Aesthetik, Halle, 1875.

STEIN, KARL HEINRICH VON
Die Entstehung der neuen Aesthetik, Stuttgart, 1886.

Meditationes philosophicae
de nonnullis
ad poema pertinentibus

MEDITATIONES PHILOSOPHICAE
DE
NONNVLLIS
AD
POEMA
PERTINENTIBVS,
QVAS
AMPLISSIMI PHILOSOPHO-
RVM ORDINIS
CONSENSV

AD D.   SEPTEMBRIS MDCCXXXV.
H. L. Q. C.

ERVDITORVM DIIVDICATIONI SVBMITTIT
M. ALEXANDER GOTTLIEB
BAVMGARTEN,
RESPONDENTE
NATHANAELE BAVMGARTEN.

HALAE MAGDEBVRGICAE,
LITTERIS IOANNIS HENRICI GRVNERTI, ACAD. TYPOG R.

(5)

Vod ab jneunte pueritia non mirifice folum vtrique noftrum arrifit ftudiorum genus; fed fuadentibus etiam, quibus obfequi par erat, fapientiffimis viris non plane negle&um eft:
in eo iam publice qualescunque noftras vires experiri conftituimus. Ex
quo enim tempore ad humanitatem
informari coeperam, incitante dexterrimo tirocinii mei
moderatore, quem fine gratiffimi animi fenfu nominare
non poffum Cl. CHRISTGAVIO gymnafii, quod Berolini floret, conre&ore meritiffimo, tranfiit mihi pæne nulla
dies fine carmine. Succrefcente paullatim aetate, licet iam
in ipfis fcholafticis fubfelliis ad feueriora magis magisque
fle&endus effet animus, & academica tandem vita prorfus alios labores, aliam diligentiam poftulare videretur:
ita tamen addixi me litteris neceffariis, vt poefi tam a caftisfima iucunditate, quam ab vtilitate præclara mihi commendatiffimae nuntium omnino mittere nunquam a me potuerim
impetrare. Inter ea contigit diuino nutu, quem veneror,

vt

vt iuuentutem ad academias maturescentem docendi poe-
ticen cum philosophia, quam vocant, rationali coniun-
ctam mihi demandaretur prouincia. Quid hic erat aequius,
quam praecepta philosophandi transferre in vsum, qua se prima nobis offerebat occasio? Quid vero indignius dicam,
an difficilius philosopho, quam iurare in verba aliorum, &
scripta magistrorum stentorea voce recitare? Accingendus
eram ad meditationem eorum, quae de more cognoueram
historice, per vsum, imitationem, nisi coecam, luscam tamen, & exspectationem casuum similium. In eo quum es-
sem mutata rerum iterum mearum facies, & conniuentibus
oculis in lucem Fridericianae protractus sum. Vehementer
abhorreo temeritatem illorum, qui cruda quaeuis & indige-
sta porriciunt in apricum, & male sedulam calamorum in-
dustriam prostituunt magis orbi litterato, quam probant.
Factum hinc esse non diffiteor, vt, quod academiarum a me
sanctissimae leges postulant, illi non prius satisfacerem offi-
cio. Nunc autem vt fiat satis, materiam eam elegi, quae
multis quidem habebitur tenuis & a philosophorum acumi-
ne remotissima, mihi videtur pro tenuitate virium mearum
satis grauis, & pro rei dignitate satis commoda ad exercen-
dos animos in inuestigandis omnium rationibus occupatos.
Vt enim ex vna, quae dudum mente haeserat, poematis notione probari plurima dicta iam centies, vix semel proba-
ta posse demonstrarem, & hoc ipso philosophiam & poematis pangendi scientiam habitas saepe pro diffitissimis ami-
micissimo iunctas connubio ponerem ob oculos, vsque ad §.
XI. in euoluenda poematis & agnatorum terminorum idea
teneor, deinde cogitationum aliquam poeticarum imaginem
animo concipere laboro a §. XIII‥LXV. post haec metho-
dum poematis lucidam, qua communis est omnibus, eruo a
§. LXV.

§. LXV.-LXXVII. tandem ad terminos poeticos conuerſus eos etiam ponderare curatius inſtituo §. LXXVII-CVII. Definitionis nóſtrae foecunditate declarata eandem conferre vi-
ſum eſt, cum nonnullis aliis, & in fine de poetica generali tria
verba ſubneĉtere. Nec plura permiſit inſtituti ratio, nec me-
ditantis imbecillitas meliora, grauiora poſthinc & maturiora
forte largientur DEVS, tempus, induſtria.

§. I.

O RATIONEM cum dicimus, *ſeriem vocum repraeſentationes*
connexas ſignificantium intelligimus.

Vnam hanc vocem teſtem citare poſſemus, ſi quis definitiones terminorum clarorum omnes inutilitatis reas ageret. Cla-
re intelligunt, qui nondum aëre lauantur, quid ſit oratio, niſi tamen
diſtinĉtus eius, quem ſequimur, ſignificatus exponatur, mens vaga fluĉtuat, & quam notionem poteſtatemue voci tribuat in prae-
ſenti, prorſus ignorat. Orationem cum meditatione & tentatio-
ne commendat Theologus, in qua tamen voce ſunt modi definitionem perperam ingreſſuri. Orationem logicus a ſchola di-
ĉtus cum ſuo Ariſtotele τον εξω λογον τον προφορικον vocat, id,
cuius partes ſignificant ſeparatim, & verminante iecinore, ſitne
ſyllogiſmus oratio, an orationes, diſquirit. Orationem magna
voce rhetor edicit ſedulo diſtinguendam a declamatione, vtne
pugnam & palaria confudiſſe videamur. Liceat communem loquendi vſum ſequutos eruere, quid illud ſit, quod latius orationem vocamus quotidie, ſi quis vero ſermonem maluerit ap-
pellare, non bella mouebimus nullos habitura triumphos. Qui
ſermones Horatii cogitarit, videbit hic aptius a termino ſermo-
nis abſtineri.

§. II. *Ex oratione repraeſentationes connexae cognoſcen-*
dae ſunt. §. 1.

Minor eſt axioma definitionis, maiorem dabit definitio ſi-
gnificantis ſiue ſigni, quae, vt ontologica ſatis nota, omittitur.

A 3

Peti-

Petimus enim hanc veniam, vt, quae inter emunctioris naris philosophos pro demonstratis & definitis habentur sine definitione, dum eandem ob oculos ponamus, sine demonstratione adhibere concedatur. Citationes hypothetice impossibiles. Demonstrationes partim aliunde transfundendae, partim non sine μεταβα-σει εις αλλο γενος essent nectendae. *Cicero Tusc. Quaest. lib. V. p. m. 250. Verumtamen mathematicorum iste mos est, non philosophorum. Nam geometrae cum aliquid docere volunt, si quid ad eam rem pertinet eorum, quae ante docuerunt, id sumunt pro concesso & probato (definito) illud modo explicant, de quo ante nihil scriptum est. Philosophi quamcunque rem habent in manibus, in eam, quae conueniunt, congerunt omnia, etsi alio loco disputata sunt.* Egregiam vero laudem & spolia ampla sophorum αγεω-μετρητων.

§. III. REPRAESENTATIONES *per partem facultatis cognoscitiuae inferiorem comparatae* sint SENSITIVAE.

Quoniam appetitus quam diu ex confusa boni repraesentatione manat, sensitiuus appellatur: confusa autem cum obscura repraesentatione comparatur per facultatis cognoscitiuae inferiorem partem, poterit idem nominis ad ipsas etiam repraesentationes applicari, vt distinguantur ita ab intellectualibus distinctis per omnes gradus possibiles.

§. IV. ORATIO *repraesentationum sensitiuarum* sit SENSITIVA.

Sicut nemo philosophorum eo profunditatis descendit, vt intellectu puro perspexisset omnia, nunquam haerens in confusa quorundam cognitione, adeoque oratio nulla paene tam est scientifica & intellectualis, vt ne vna quidem occurrat per omnem nexum sensitiua idea, ita potest etiam distinctae praesertim cognitioni dans operam inuenire has vel illas repraesentationes distinctas in oratione sensitiua, manet tamen sensitiua, vt prior abstracta & intellectualis.

§. V. *Ex oratione sensitiua repraesentationes sensitiuae connexae cognoscendae sunt.* §. 2. 4.

§. VI.

§. VI. *Orationis fenfitiuae varia funt* 1) *repraefentatio-nes fenfitiuae*, 2) *nexus earum*, 3) *voces fiue foni articulati litte-ris conftantes earum figna.* §. 4.1.

§. VII. ORATIO SENSITIVA PERFECTA *eft*, *cuius varia tendunt ad cognitionem repraefentationum fenfitiuarum.*§.5.

§. VIII. *Quo plura varia in oratione fenfitiua facient ad excitandas repraefentationes fenfitiuas, eo erit illa perfectior.* §. 4.7.

§. IX. *Oratio fenfitiua perfecta eft* POEMA, *complexus regularum, ad quas conformandum poema* POETICE, *fcientia po-etices* PHILOSOPHIA POETICA, *habitus conficiendi poema-tis* POESIS, *eoque habitu gaudens* POETA.

In recoquendis harum vocum, quas fcholaftici dicunt, defi-nitionibus nominalibus patent compilanda Scaligerorum, Voffio-rum plurimorumque refertiffima fcrinia. Libentes tamen manum de tabula, fi hoc vnum monuerimus. Poema & poefin cum Lu-cilio, Nonius Marcellus, Aphthonius, Donatus videntur diftin-guere tantum, vt maius & minus, & poefeos i. e. longioris cuius-dam poematis, poema facere partem aliquam & fectionem, vt dif-ferant, ficut Ilias & nauium graecarum catalogus apud Homerum. In quo tamen a Voffio iam oppofitus illis eft vfus.

Quem penes arbitrium eft & ius & norma loquendi.

Quando tamen idem Ciceronem concedit vti termino poefeos lo-co poematis, omne punctum vix feret. Citata enim loca contra-rium innuere videntur: Quaeft.Tufcul.l. V. p.m. 269. quum Home-ro non poefin fed picturam tribuit, artem omnia & ea, quae fub ocu-los cadunt, imitandi in coeco miratur, non vero huius artis effe-ctum, faltim non exclufiue, quod tamen neceffarium effet. fi hinc in-folitus vocis poefeos fignificatus probari poffet. Aliter locus non in libro VI. vt in duabus Vosfii editionibus fcriptum legitur, fed in IV. Quaeft. Tufcul. p. m. 243. poefin anacreontis totam effe di-cit amatoriam. An vero hic queat fubftitui vox poema in nume-ro fingulari: an potius omnem fundendorum carminum impetum apud Anacreontem ad amores cauendos vnice propendere doceat
Cicero

Cicero, & poefis ita retineat vindicatam ipfi poteftatem, non difficulter, nifi fallimur, poterit diiudicari.

§. X. *Poematis varia* funt, *1) repraefentationes fenfitiuae 2) earum nexus 3) voces earum figna.* §. 9. 6.

§. XI. POETICVM dicetur *quicquid ad perfectionem poematis aliquid facere poteft.*

§. XII. Repraefentationes fenfitiuae funt varia poematis §. 10. ergo poeticae §. 11. 7. quum autem fenfitiuae aut obfcurae aut clarae §. 3. fint, *obfcurae et clarae funt repraefentationes poeticae.*

Poffunt quidem eiusdem rei repraefentationes huic obfcurae, illi clarae, tertio denique diftinctae effe, quando vero de repraefentationibus oratione fignificandis fermo eft, eae intelliguntur, quas loquens intendit communicare. Hic ergo quaeritur, quas poeta in poemate fignificare repraefentationes intendat.

§. XIII. In repraefentationibus obfcuris non tot continentur notarum repraefentationes, quot ad recognofcendum & diftinguendum ab aliis repraefentatum fufficiunt, continentur vero in repraefentationibus claris (per deff.) ergo plura varia facient ad communicandas repraefentationes fenfitiuas, eae, fi fuerint clarae, quam fi fuerint obfcurae. Ergo poema, cuius repraefentationes clarae, perfectius, quam cuius obfcurae, & *clarae repraefentationes magis poeticae* §. 11. *quam obfcurae.*

Hinc eorum refutatur error, qui quo obfcurius & intricatius effutire poffunt, hoc fe loqui fomniant ποητικωτερως. Neutiquam vero pedibus itur in illorum fententiam, qui optimos quosque poetas ideo reiectum eunt, quia oculis male inunctis meras fe ibi tenebras fpiffamque videre noctem arbitrantur. e. g. Perfii Sat. IV. v. 45. 46.

Si Puteal multa cautus vibice flagellas
Nequicquam populo bibulas donaueris aures.

notam cimmeriae caligualis inuret temere hiftoriae Neronianae ignarus,

rus, quam qui contulerit aut latina nescit, aut sensum assequitur, & satis claras repraesentationes experitur.

§. XIV. *Repraesentationes distinctae,* completae, adaequatae, profundae per omnes gradus *non* sunt sensitiuae ergo nec *poeticae.'*§. II.

A posteriori experiundo patescet veritas, si talibus repraesentationibus praegnantes praelegantur versiculi homini philosopho simulque poeseos non prorsus ignaro: quales e. gr.

> *Quum qui demonstrant alios errasse, refutent,*
> *Nemo refutabit, nisi demonstretur ab illo*
> *Erratum alterius: Qui demonstrare iubetur*
> *Hunc logicam sciuisse decet, quicunque refutat*
> *Ergo, tamen logicus non est, non rite refutat.* per vers. I.

vix admittet eos omnibus numeris absolutos, licet ipse fortean ignoret, quam ob caussam sibi reiiciendi videantur nec in forma, nec in materia peccantes. Haec autem est praecipua ratio, cur philosophia et poesis vix vnquam in vna sede morari posse putentur, illa maximopere sectante conceptuum distinctionem, quam haec tamen extra suos circulos ascendentem non curat. Si quis tamen in vtraque faeultatis cognoscitiuae parte excellat, & quamlibet suo adhibere loco didicerit, nae, ille sine alterius detrimento ad alteram exasciandam incumbet, & Aristotelem, Leibnitium eum sexcentis aliis pallium lauro iungentibus fuisse sentiet prodigia, non miracula.

§. XV. Quum clarae *repraesentationes* sint *poeticae* §. 13. aut erunt distinctae aut confusae, iam distinctae non sunt §. 14. ergo *confusae.*

§. XVI. *Si in repraesentatione A plura repraesententur, quam in B. C. D. &c. sint tamen omnes confusae,* A erit reliquis EXTENSIVE CLARIOR.

Addenda fuit restrictio, vt distinguerentur hi claritatis gradus a satis cognitis illis, qui per notarum distinctionem descendunt ad cognitionis profunditatem, & vnam repraesentationem altera intensiue reddunt clariorem.

B

§. XVII.

§. XVII. In extensiue clarisfimis repraesentationibus plura repraesentantur sensitiue, quam in minus claris §. 16. ergo plura faciunt ad perfectionem poematis §. 7. Hinc *repraesentationes extensiue clariores sunt maxime poeticae* §. 11.

§. XVIII. Quo magis res determinantur, hoc repraesentationes earum plura complectuntur; quo vero plura in repraesentatione confusa cumulantur, hoc fit extensiue clarior §. 16. magisque poetica §. 17. Ergo *in poemate res repraesentandas quantum pote, determinari poeticum* §. 11.

§. XIX. Indiuidua sunt omnimode determinata, ergo *repraesentationes singulares sunt admodum poeticae* §. 18.

Nostris Choerilis tantum abest, vt obseruetur haec poematis elegantia, vt potius naso adunco suspendant Homerum Il. β. ηγεμονας και κοιρανας, αρχας αυνηων νηας τε προπασας dicentem, narrantem Il. η. omnes, Hectori qui obuiam ire sustinebant, in Hymno autem Apollinis plurima regnantis dei loca sacra recensentem. Idem in Virgilii Aneide, qui libr. VII. finem & posteriores euoluerit satis superque notare poterit. Addatur & Ouidii catalogus canum dominum lacerantium in Metamorphosi, nec quisquam, puto, concipere poterit non opinantibus aut inuitis excidisse, quae nobis imitatu difficillima forent.

§. XX. Ad genus cum determinationes specificae accedentes constituant speciem & genus inferius ad genus superius adiectae determinationes genericae, *generis inferioris & speciei repraesentationes magis poeticae, quam generis, aut generis superioris,* §. 18.

Ne videamur probationem a posteriori quaesitam anxie arcessere longius prima prodeat oda Venusini lyrici. Cur in ea *ataui* pro maioribus, *puluis olympicus* pro puluere ludorum, *palma* pro praemio, *Lybicae areae* pro terris frugiferis, *Attalicae conditiones* pro magnis, *trabs Cypria* pro mercatoria, *mare myrtoum* pro periculoso, *luctans Icariis fluctibus Africus* pro vento, *vetus Massicum* pro vino generoso, *Marsus* aper pro fulmineo &c.

nisi

nifi virtutis effet fubftituere conceptibus latioribus anguftiores. Nihil dicemus de ipfa difpofitione totius odae hac ratione inftituta, vt pro ambitione, auaritia & voluptate adducantur fpecialiores cafus, in quibus fe iftae folent exferere : & amplificatione omni hinc dedu&a , vt pro pluribus cafibus fimilibus gencraliori titulo donandis exprimatur vnus & alter verf. 26. 27. 33. 34. Tibullus pro aromatis fuo cineri infundendis libr. III. tres aromatum fpecies poftulat

> *Illic quas mittit diues Pænebaia merces*
> *Eoique Arabes, diues & Affyria*, §. 19.
> *Et noftri memores lacrumae fundantur eodem.*

Maro pro: nunquam hoc faciam, nota circumfcriptione poetarum di&urus :

> *Cun&a prius fiunt, fieri quae poffe negabam,*
> *Naturaeque prius contraria legibus ibunt.*

Ecl. I. defcendit ad enumerationem fpecialiorem phyfice impoffibilium quorundam rufticis notiffimorum :

> *Ante leues - - pafcentur in aethere cerui &c.*

Ex eodem hoc fonte fluit diftributio poetica,vbi de pluribus loquuturi poetae ftatim ea in claffes & fpecies folent difpertiri. Notum Virgilii illud de Troadibus in Lybiam adie&is Aen. libr. I.   It. in Catullo c. 58, Satyros & Nifigenas Silenos repraefentaturo :

> *Horum pars te&a quatiebat cufpide thyrfoi*

& verf. fqq. 8. fpecies diuerfa agentium enarrantur.

§. XXI.   EXEMPLVM *eft repraefentatio magis determinati ad declarandam repraefentationem minus determinati fuppeditata.*

Quum nondum relatam alibi legimus hanc definitionem, cum vfu loquendi eam optime conuenire probaturi fumimus arithmeticum afferentem: aequalibus quantitatibus aequales additas aequalia aggregata producere,feu: fi $A = Z$. $B = Y$. $A + B = Z + Y$. Iam loco numeri indeterminati A fi fubftituat determinatum 4 loco Z 2 + 2 loco B. 6. loco Y 3 + 3 & 4 + 6 $=$ 2 + 2 + 3 + 3 iuret, exemplum fui axiomatis dediffe dicetur omni-

bus

bus eo fi fine factum fit, vt clarius patefcat, quod literalibus fuis
fibi velit characteribus. Philofophus improprias locutiones exfu-
lare debere ex definitione demonftraturus, fi cum Campanella *febrim*
definiat per *bellum contra morbum poteftatiua vi fpiritus initum,*
aut fpiritus fpontaneam extraordinariam agitationem inflammatio-
nemque ad pugnam contra irritantem morbificam cauffam: vt hinc
tales definitiones eo penitius introfpiciantur, exemplum definitionis impropriae dediffe creditur, dum loco definitionis in genere
protulit aliquod indiuiduum, & loco conceptus generalis de impropriis loquutionibus repraefentauit bellum, fpiritus agitationem
& inflammationem &c. &c. conceptus, in quibus plura funt determinata quam effe terminum improprium, qui tamen eruendae huic
& declarandae notioni tantum adhibentur.   Foecundam effe definitionem noftram experietur, qui hinc foluere nitetur problema:
quomodo aedificans aliis exemplum praeeundum, aut meditatus
grauiffima B. SPENERI verba, quando in *conf. theol. lat. part. I. c. II.*
art. I. Mathefin affirmat *fua certitudine & demonftrationum* ασφα-
λεια *omnibus aliis fcientiis exemplum praebere, quod, quantum fieri*
poteft, imitentur. coll. §. 107.

§. XXII.   *Exempla confufe repraefentata* funt repraef-
fentationes extenfiue clariores, *quam eae, quibus declarandis*
proponuntur §. 21. hinc *magis poeticae* §. 18. & *in exemplis fingu-*
laria quidem *optima* §. 19.

     Id, quod vidit Ill. LEIBNITZIVS egregio illo libro, quo
cauffam Dei defendendam fufcepit Part. II. p. 148. quando ait: *Le*
but principal de la Poefie doit etre d' enfeigner la prudence & la
vertu par des exemples. Exemplum exempli dum quaerimus, paene facti fumus Tantali in tanta affluentia, vnde potiffimum hau-
riendum incerti.   Decurramus ad mare miferi Nafonis Trift. l. I.
& II. minus determinata repraefentatio:

      Saepe premente deo fert deus alter opem.

vix elapfa erat ex ore falfis lacrumarum & maris imbribus rorante:
& ecce repente fequitur 6 verfibus fibi vindicans exemplorum decu-
manus fluctus

     Mulciber in Troiam pro Troia ftabat Achilles &c.

                              §. XXIII.

§. XXIII. *Conceptus A, qui praeter notas conceptus B cum ipso repraesentatur, ipsi* ADHAERET, *& cui alius adhaeret*, dicitur CONCEPTVS COMPLEXVS, oppofitus SIMPLICI, *cui nullus adhaeret*. Conceptus complexus quum plura, quam fimplex repraefentet, *conceptus complexi confufi* funt extenfiue clariores, quam fimplices §. 16. hinc *magis poetici, quam fimplices*. §. 17.

§. XXIV. REPRAESENTATIONES *mutationum repraefentantis praefentium* funt SENSVALES, eaeque fenfiti·uae §. 3. adeoque *poeticae* §. 12.

§. XXV. Affectus cum fint notabiliores taedii & voluptatis gradus, dantur eorum repraefentationes fenfuales in repraefentante fibi quid confufe, vt bonum & malum, ergo determinant repraefentationes poeticas §. 24. ergo *affectus mouere eft poeticum*. §. 11.

§. XXVI. Idem & hac ratione demonftrari poteft: quae repraefentantur, vt bona nobis & mala, in iis plura nobis repraefentantur, quam fi non ita repraefentarentur, ergo repraefentationes rerum, quae vt bonae malaeue nobis confufe offeruntur, extenfiue clariores, quam fi ita non proponerentur §. 16. hinc magis poeticae §. 17. Tales vero repraefentationes funt motiones affectuum, ergo *mouere affectus poeticum* §. 11.

§. XXVII. *Senfiones fortiores* funt clariores, ergo *magis poeticae*, quam minus clarae, & *imbecilles* §. 17. fenfiones fortiores comitantur affectum vehementiorem, quam minus vehementem §. 25. Ergo excitare affectus vehementiffimos maxime poeticum. Idem hinc patet. Quae nobis aut vt peffima, aut vt optima confufe repraefentantur, extenfiue clarius repraefentantur, quam fi vt minus bona minusue mala repraefentarentur §. 16. & hinc magis poetice §. 17. Iam re-

B 3   prae·

praefentatio confufa rei vt nobis peffimae aut optimae de-
terminat affectus vehementiffimos.   Ergo *affectus vehemen-
tiores excitare magis poeticum, quam minus vehementes.*

§. XXVIII.   *Phantafmata* funt repraefentationes fenfitiuae §. 3. adeoque *poeticae* §. 12.

  Quum hic repraefentationes fenforum reproductas phantafmata vocamus: recedimus quidem cum philofophis a vaga figni-
ficatione vocis, nequè tamen ab vfu loquendi & ipfis regulis grammaticis, quis enim negaret phantafma effe, quod imaginati fumus?
Iam vero facultas imaginandi in ipfo Suidae lexico defcribitur tanquam παρα της αισθησεως λαμβανεσα των αισθητων τας τυπας, εν
αυτη τετας αναπλατίων.   Quid ergo phantafmata, nifi refictae
(reproductae) fenfualium imagines (repraefentationes) a fenfatione
acceptae, quod iam indicatur conceptu fenfualium?

§. XXIX.   Phantafmata minus clara quam ideae fenfuales, Ergo minus poetica §. 17.   Quum ergo affectus mo-
ti determinant ideas fenfuales, poema mouens affectus perfectius quam plenum phantafmafi mortuis §. 8. 9. & *affectus
mouere magis poeticum, quàm phantafmata alia producere.*

  *Non fatis eft pulchra effe poemata - -
  Et quocunque volent, animum auditoris agunto.*
Bellum fane characterem, quo
  Corui poetae cum poetriis picis
& Homeri dignofcantur facillime, illis plerumque *magna profeffis*
  Purpureus, late qui fplendeat, vnus & alter
  Affuitur pannus.
ergo non omnino damnat ifta Flaccus; videamus tamen quaenam
fint, de quibus caute adhibendis poeta loquatur fungens vice co-
tis :

  - - - - cum lucus & arca Dianae (phantafma 1. & 2.)
  Aut flumen Rhenum (phant. 3.) *aut pluuius defcribitur
       arcus* (phant. 4.)
  Sed nunc non erat his locus.

               Iam

Iam secundum §. 22. quum agat poeta, ex his speciebus & magis determinatis, tanquam exemplis, euoluamus notionem magis vniuersalem, nulla sane reperietur, in qua conueniant, quam notio phantasmatum, phantasmati ergo non semper locus, rationem §. suppeditat.   Quare, si cum Flacco sentiam, *faber vngues exprimens & molles aere capillos imitans* (quaedam phantasmata in carmine apte repraesentans.)

>   *Infelix operis summa*
>   *Non magis esse velim, quam prauo viuere naso*
>   *Spectandus nigris oculis, nigroque capillo.*

§. XXX.   Phantasmate partiali repraesentato, phantasma eius totale recurrit, & eius adeo constituit conceptum complexum, qui si confusus fuerit, erit magis poeticus, quam simplex §. 23.   Ergo *cum phantasmate partiali totale repraesentare, idque extensiue clarius* §. 17. *est poeticum.*

§. XXXI.   *Ratione loci & temporis coexistentia* phantasmati partiali pertinent cum eo ad idem totale, ergo eorum phantasmata extensiue clara *cum repraesentando aliquo partiali repraesentare, poeticum* §. 30.

Vsitatissimae poetis descriptiones temporis e. g. noctis Virgil. Aen. IV. meridiei Ecl. 4. vesperae Ecl. 1. quatuor anni horas simul depictas lege in Senecae Hippol. Act. III. p. 64. descriptiones veris Virg. Georg. l. II. vers. 319 - 345. primae lucis, hiemis, autumni &c. & alia exempla cuiuslibet Bauii aduersaria porrigent.   In quibus tamen maximopere obseruandum scholion ad §. 28.

§. XXXII.   Ratione loci & temporis repraesentando coexistentia phantasmati poetice simul repraesentari & hac ratione demonstrari potest: res, quantum pote, determinatissimas repraesentari poeticum §. 18. determinationes loci & temporis numericae, saltim specificae, ergo rem maxime determinant, ergo repraesentare omnia, ergo &

phan-

phantafmata indicando coexiftentia per locum & tempus determinare poeticum.

§. XXXIII. Repraefentato phantafmate certae fpeciei vel generis, recurrunt *phantafmata alia eiusdem fpeciei vel generis, fi* talia *cum genere vel fpecie fimul repraefententur, partim fit illud conceptus* complexus confufus, hinc *magis poeticus* §. 23. *partim* magis determinatur *genus vel fpecies* & hinc *repraefentatur magis poetice.* §. 20. 19.

§. XXXIV. Si cum repraefentando phantafmate fpecies vel genus, quod cum aliis commune habet, fimul repraefentetur confufe, fit extenfiue clarius, quam fi hoc non factum fit §. 16. hinc *genus & fpeciem, quae repraefentandum phantafma cum aliis communia habet repraefentare poeticum.* §. 17.

§. XXXV. Si talia, quae ad genus idem & eandem fpeciem repraefentandam cum phantafmate quodam pertinent, fimul repraefententur, genus repraefentatur magis poetice, quam fi fecus factum fit §. 33. Iam genus vel fpecies repraefentare cum repraefentando phantasmate poeticum §. 34. Ergo *cum phantafmate repraefentando repraefentare etiam phantafmata ad idem genus fiue eandem fpeciem pertinentia admodum poeticum.*

§. XXXVI. SIMILIA funt, *quibus idem conuenit conceptus fuperior,* ergo fimilia ad eandem fpeciem vel genus idem pertinent. Ergo *cum repraefentando phantafmate vno repraefentare fimilia admodum poeticum.* §. 35.

Atque adeo patet etiam ratio, cur fimilia tantis exigant clamoribus, qui pythia cantaturos formant fub ferula magiftri. Effe vero hanc in fimilia delabendi proniffimam viam patebit ex exemplo Didonis apud Maronem libr I. templum Iunonis ingredientis, habet hic poeta mulierem caeteris comitantibus multis praeftan-

praeftantem in fummo ornatu, hae conftituunt notae fimul fum-
tae fpeciem, fub eadem continetur Diana, & ecce, Diana hic fit
fimile, fimile enim eft non exemplum licet a perfona defumtum
fit. §. 17.

§. XXXVII. *Repraefentationes fomniorum* funt phantafmata, ergo *poeticae* §. 28.

Deprehendimus eas in Virgilio, Ouidio, Tibullo at quibus
caftae Poefeos arbitris? Adeoque non omnino reiiciendae, licet
bilem vtique moueant vates, vrget fane

Quos fanaticus error & iracunda Diana,

vt nihil nifi fomniorum interpretamenta nouerint exponere, quo-
ties Caius Caiam duxit, aut obfcurum nefcio quod microcofmi lu-
men extinctum eft.

§. XXXVIII. Quo *phantafmata* clarius repraefentantur, eo magis fiunt fenfualibus ideis fimilia, ita vt debi-
liori fenfationi faepe aequipolleant. Iam phantafmata repraefentare, quam fieri poteft clariffime, poeticum §.17. ergo ea *fenfationibus facere fimillima poeticum.*

§. XXXIX. Picturae eft repraefentare compofi-
tum idem & poeticum §. 24. picturae repraefentatio pingen-
di fenfuali eius ideae fimillima, idem poeticum §.38. Ergo
poema & pictura fimilia §. 30.

Vt pictura, poefis erit.

In hoc enim loco concedere iubet hermeneutica quaedam necesfi-
tas confequentia conferentem poefin pro poemate pofitam & picturam non de arte fed effectu intelligendam. Neque tamen hinc
ambigendum eft de genuina poefeos notione *§.* 9. rite fixa & con-
ftituta, in talibus enim verborum paene fynonymicorum confu-
fionibus & poetis aliis & noftro

Quidlibet audendi femper fuit aequa poteftas.

§. XL. Pictura cum reprafentet phantafma in fu-
perficie tantum, eius non eft omnem fitum vllumque mo-
tum repraefentare, fed eft poeticum, quia his etiam reprae-

C   fentatis sentatis plura in obiecto repraesentantur, quam non repraesentatis iis, & hinc fit illud extensiue clarius § 16. Ergo in imaginibus poeticis plura ad vnum tendunt quam in pictis. Hinc *perfectius poema pictura.*

§. XLI.   Vocum & orationis quanquam clariora phantasmata, quam visibilium, hinc tamen praerogatiuam poematis prae pictura affirmare non conamur, quoniam intensiua claritas cognitioni per voces symbolicae concessa prae intuitiua nihil facit ad extensiuam claritatem, quae sola poetica. §. 17. 14.

      Verum illud per experientiam & §. 29.

         Segnius irritant animos demissa per aurem
         Quam quae sunt oculis subiecta fidelibus, & quae
         Ipse sibi tradit spectator. - -

§. XLII.   *Confusa repraesentationis cognitio* est memoriae sensitiua, hinc sensitiua §. 3. & *poetica* §. 12.

§. XLIII.   ADMIRATIO est *intuitus plurium in repraesentatione tanquam non contentorum in multis perceptionum nostrarum seriebus.*

      Conuenimus cum Cartesio admirationem habente pro *subitanea animae occupatione, qua fertur in considerationem attentam obiectorum, quae ipsi videntur rara & extraordinaria,* ita tamen vt reiectis, quae videntur superflua, ad demonstrationis seriem definitionem accommodemus   Quum raritatem in mirabilibus solam male videatur requirere nonnullis, exclusa ignoratione, non ipsi quidem dicam scribemus iterum, sed in extraordinario potius implicite dici inconceptibile relatiuum sentimus, nihilo tamen secius vtrumque admirationis fontem clare indicasse laborauimus.

§. XLIV.   Quum intuitiua cognitio possit esse confusa, potest esse & admiratio §. 43. hinc *repraesentatio mirabilium poetica* §. 13.

                                            §. XLV.

§. XLV.   Ad ea, in quibus mirabilia, attendere folemus, ad quae attendimus, ea ficonfufe, extenfiue clarius repraefentantur, quam ad quae non attendimus §. 16. ergo *repraefentationes, in quibus mirabilia, magis poeticae, quam in quibus non funt.*

> Hinc Horatius:
>> *Fauete linguis.   Carmina non prius*
>> *Audita Mufarum facerdos*
>> *Virginibus puerisque canto.*

Forte & haec innuuntur, fi ex allegoria euoluantur cogitata eiusdem in Oda 20. libr. II. vbi incipit:

>> *Non vfitata, nec tenui ferar*
>> *Penna - - - -*

Regeritur haec non materiam, fed formam carminis lyrici in Latio ante Horatium incultioris refpicere.   Verum fit ita; non excluditur tamen materia, &, fi excluditur, per ipfam formam mirabilem excitat fecundum §.' repraefentationes poeticas.   Et quum in ipfo limine gloriae auidus id profiteatur, habuit fane pro laude poetae *non vfitata, non audita prius* dicere, quod volumus vnum.

§. XLVI.   *Vbi admiratio, ibi plura* non confufe recognita §. 43.   Ergo *minus poetice repraefentata.* § 42.

Vbi recognitio confufa, ibi ceffare admirationem a pofteriore etiam conftare poteft, fi quem videmus quippiam mirari e. g. inftrumentum bellicum artificiofe confectum, alter ipfum in admirando impediturus quaerit, annon eadem, immo artificiofiora, viderit Berolini, Dresdae e. c.   Quod fi reminifcitur, vtique remittit admiratio.

§. XLVII.   Mirabilium repraefentatio poetica §. 45. alioque refpectu non talis §. 46. hinc regularum conflictus & neceffaria exceptio.

§. XLVIII.   Quod fi ergo mirabilia repraefentanda §. 45. debent tamen quaedam in eorum repraefentatione pos-

C 2   fe

fe confufe recognofci, i. e. *in ipfis mirabilibus nota incognitis apte mifcere maxime poeticum* §. 47.

§. XLIX. *Miracula* quum fint actiones indiuiduales *admodum poeticae* eorum *repraefentationes* §. 19. quum tamen rariffime fiant in regno naturae, faltim percipiantur vt talia, mirabilia funt §. 43. hinc nota & facillima recognitu iptis interferenda §. 48.

> *Ne deus interfit, nifi dignus vindice nodus*
> *Inciderit.*

Ex poematis notione, quam §. 9. exhibitam tuemur, narrandorum miraculorum libertas fluit, confirmata exemplis optimorum poetarum innumeris, quae tamen videtur in licentiam degenerare, fi poema hoc vnum fibi propofitum habeat, vt naturam imitetur. Naturae nempe nihil cum miraculis.

§. L. *Repraefentationes confufae ex diuifis & compofitis phantafmafi natae* funt phantafmata, ergo *poeticae* § 23.

§. LI. *Repraefentationum talium obiecta vel in mundo exiftente posfibilia vel imposfibilia.* Has FIGMENTA, illas liceat dicere FIGMENTA VERA.

§. LII. *Figmentorum obiecta vel in exiftente tantum, vel in omnibus mundis poffibilibus impoffibilia, haec* quae VTOPICA dicemus abfolute impoffibilia, *illa* falutabimus HETEROCOSMICA. Ergo *vtopicorum nulla,* hinc nec confufa, nec *poetica datur repraefentatio.*

§. LIII. *Sola figmenta vera & heterocofmica funt poetica* §. 50. 52.

§. LIV. DESCRIPTIONES funt *enumerationes variorum in repraefentato quorumcunque.* Quodfi ergo confufe repraefentatum defcribatur, plura in eo varia repraefentantur, quam fi non defcribatur. Quod fi CONFVSE DESCRIBATVR i. e. *repraefentationes variorum in defcribendo confufae fuppeditentur,* fit extenfiue clarius, idque, quo plura varia

varia confuse repraefentantur, hoc magis §. 16. Ergo *de-fcriptiones confufae & eae maxime, in quibus plura varia repraefentantur, maximopere poeticae.*

§. LV. *Defcriptiones idearum fenfualium, phantafmatum, figmentorum verorum & heterocofmicorum confufae funt admodum poeticae* §. 54.

Iam eximi poteft ille fcrupulus , qui haerere poffet animo cogitanti defcriptionem effe per defin. in A diftinguere B. C. D. adeoque A diftincte repraefentari,quod quum fit contra conceptum poematis §. 9. & inde fluentem §. 14. inde deduci poffe abfurdum defcriptiones ex poemate effe eliminandas. Nam B. C. D. &c.{funt fenfitiuae repraefentationes, quum confufae fupponantur §. 3. Ergo defcriptio loco vnius A fenfitiuae fubftituit B. C. D. i. e. plures fenfitiuas. Hinc licet A prorfus fieret diftinctum, quod tamen raro fit, nihilo poema minus poft defcriptionem admiffam fieret perfectius, quam ante eandem §. 8.

§. LVI. Quum *in figmentis heterocofmicis* plura, quae nec idearum fenfualium, nec phantafmatum non fictorum, nec figmentorum verorum feriem in animis multorum auditorum lectorumue ingreffa praefumi poffunt, praefumuntur mirabilia § 43. Ergo plura in iis confuse recognofcibilia fi occurrant *maxime poetice repraefentantur mifcentia nota incognitis* §. 48.

Hinc Horatius: *ex noto fictum carmen fequar*, & idem fingentem ficturus & docturus:

Quid deceat, quid non? quo virtus, quo ferat error?
Vnde parentur opes, quid alat formetue poetam?

famam fequi iubet & *Achillem reponere* i. e. fecundum § 17. Heroas materias fabularum notiffimas. *Medea, Io, Ino, Ixion, Oreftes* exempla eiusdem conceptus generalioris perfonarum in theatris triftiffimarum. Poftea expreffis verbis:

Rectius Iliacum carmen deducis in actus,
Quam fi proferres ignota indictaque primus.

C 3 Nouimus

Nouimus loqui poetam de focco coenaque Thyeftae, verum quum
ratio hanc regulam determinans fit fecundum demonftrata vniuerfalis, vniuerfalis etiam regula. Iliacum vero carmen iterum exemplum eft figmenti heterocofmici iam cogniti. *Perfonam forma-*
re nouam vocat audaciam.

§. LVII. Figmenta, in quibus plura fibi inuicem
repugnant, funt vtopica, non heterocofmica §. 52. hinc *in*
figmentis poeticis nil fibi inuicem repugnat. §. 53.
Sibi conuenientia finge.
vt de te dici queat etiam quod de Homero :

Hic ita mentitur, fic veris falfa remifcet,
Primo ne medium, medio ne difcrepet imum.
Nec, quodcunque volet, pofcat fibi fabula credi,
Neu lamiae viuum pranfae puerum extrabat aluo.
Quaecunque oftendis mihi fic, incredulus odi.
Centuriaeque agitant feniorum expertia frugis.

§. LVIII. Si philofophica vel vniuerfalia quaeuis
repraefentanda poetice, determinare quam maxime §. 18.
exemplis inuoluere §. 22. eaque ratione loci & temporis §.
28. & enumeratis aliis quam pluribus variis defcribere §.
49. mens eft; experientia non fufficiente figmenta vera,
nec hiftoria quidem fatis diuite, figmenta probabiliter heterocosmica neceffaria §. 44. 47. Ergo *figmenta tam vera,*
quam heterocosmica in poemate hypothetice neceffaria.

Quanta cum diffenfione poetarum rhetores anquirant, an
fictio ad effentialia poematis pertineat, nec ne, qui quosdam faltim euoluerit, ignorare putamus neminem. Satisfactum itaque
iuimus dubitationi in neutras omnino partes concedendo, fed de-
terminando potius certos cafus, in quibus fictione poeta fuperfe-
dere nequeat. Effe autem non dabiles folum, fed faepius etiam
obuios, experientia docet. Quum enim, ʾanquam. ciuitatis diui-
nae, quotaecunque portiones, obligemur ad talia carminibus con-
fignanda, quae virtutem & religionem promouent: factumque
illud etiam fit per omnes fere temporum viciffitudines, (vid. fub
prae-

praefidio Ioh. Andr. Schmidii habita Helmftadii differtatio *de modo propagandi religionem per carmina*) perfectionem vero veram
humani generis tam perfecte quam imperfecte reftituentia vniuerfalia fint plerumque , de vinuerfalibus etiam & minus determinatis faepiffime poetis verba facienda funt.   Hinc Horatius iam
  Rem tibi Socraticae poterunt oftendere chartae.
poffibilis ergo prima hypothefis , alterius etiam poffibilitatem videbit cogitans poetam omnibus faepe fcribere, faltim fibi ignotis,
ergo nefcit etiam , quid illorum ferat experientia , quod fi vero
phantafmata non ficta proponit, quae auditor lectorue non fenfit,
funt ifti illa figmenta vera. §. 41.   Hiftoria recentiffima, quae maxime determinata folet effe cognita , inutilis plerumque poetae
propter adulationis irrifionisque fcopulos , aut certe notam , vix
ac ne vix quidem vitandam, Hiftoria remotior nunquam tam determinate cognita, vt ftilus pofcit poeticus, per demonftrata, ergo magis determinanda, quae narrat.   Determinationes poemati
addendae, de quibus tacet hiftoria, cognofci nequeunt, nifi ex per-
fpicientia omnium requifitorum ad veritatem earundem,quae cum
in limitatum non cadat intellectum, ex aliquibus & pauciffimis rationibus infufficientiffimis hariolandae funt, adeoque vehementer
improbabilis earum veritas i. e. probabilis non exiftentia & ftatio
inter heterocofmica figmenta.

§ LIX.   Probabilia quum fieri faepius,quam improbabilia, percipiamus, *poema fingens probabilia facta magis poeti-
tice res repraefentat, quam fingens improbabilia* §. 56.

  Regni figmentorum laudabilium, quantum quantum fit, di-
minuitur tamen in dies territorium prolatis fanae rationis pomoe-
riis. Sapientiffimi quondam poetarum dici non poteft, quot vtopica figmenta contra §. 47. immifcuerint, deorum adulterorum
&c. Senfim rideri coepta funt ifta,& nunc non aperta folum con-
tradictio fingenti vitanda, fed etiam rationis defectus, aut contra
rationem fictus effectus, toties occinente poeta:
  Spectatoris eges aulaea manentis & vfque
  Seffuri, donec cantor: vos plaudite, dicat?
  Aetatis cuiusque notandi funt tibi mores.

                                                            hi

minantur per illud, non conneftuntur cum eo, nexus vero eft poticus §. 65.

Iam pofiti limites inieftaque fraena phantafiae & indomitae ingeniorum lafciuiae, quae abuti mifere poffet §§. prioribus, phantafmata & figmenta in poema non admittentibus folum, fed & ad perfeftionem poftulantibus. Nunc enim videmus: fint in abftrafto licet omnino bonae repraefentationes, tamen in coordinando reieftum iri omnem ideam fenfualem, omne figmentum, omne phantafma,

Quod non propofito (themati) *conducat & haereat apte.*
Dudum obferuatum, poetam quafi faftorem fiue creatorem effe, hinc poema effe debet quafi mundus Hinc κατ' αναλογιαν de eodem tenenda, quae de mundo philofophis patent.

§. LXIX. Si determinentur repraefentationes poeticae, quae non themata, per thema, conneftuntur cum themate, ergo conneftuntur inter fe, ergo fibi inuicem fuccedunt, vt cauffa & cauffatum, ergo fimilitudo obferuabilis in modo, quo fibi fuccedunt, adeoque in poemate eft ordo. Iam connefti repraefentationes poeticas, quae non themata, cum themate poeticum §. 69. ergo *ordo eft poeticus.*

§. LXX. Quum ordo in repraefentationum fucceffione dicatur methodus, *methodus eft poetica* §. 69. eam vero METHODVM, quae poetica, dicamus, cum poeta *lucidum ordinem* poetis tribuente, LVCIDAM.

§. LXXI. Methodi lucidae generalis regula eft: *ita fe excipiant repraefentationes poeticae, vt thema extenfiue clarius fenfim clariusque repraefentetur.* Quum thema proponendum fenfitiue §. 9. intenditur eius claritas extenfiua §. 17. quod fi iam antecedentes clarius repraefentantur, quam fequentes repraefentationes, pofteriores non concurrunt ad illud poetice repraefentandum, debent tamen concurrere §. 68. ergo *pofteriores clarius reddere debent thema, quam priores.*

In

In primo poematum limine iam olim ob hanc neglectam methodi regulam fibi videbantur veteres iure ridere cyclicos illos poetas, quorum fimul ac calamum ftringunt

> *Parturiunt montes.*

Quis non damnat *immanes hiatus fublimes verfus ructantium* quorum pegafeum oeftrum, poftquam fe vix fronte caballino proluerunt, in ipfo adhuc portu

> *Proiicit ampullas & fesquipedalia verba.*

Non Lucano, Statio, aliis diem dicemus iterum male iam mulcatis a pluribus ob hoc vitium.   Praeftare videbatur partim rationem dare, quam ob rem finiftre coepta fic coepta fint carmina; partim extendere regulam, contra quam impegerunt ifti, ad omnem poematis decurfum.   Vbique feruandum illud, quod in Homero tantam laudem mereri iudicat Horatius:

> *Quanto*, inquiens, *rectius hic, qui nil molitur inepte.*
> *Non fumum ex fulgore, fed ex fumo dare lucem*
> *Cogitat, vt fpeciofa dehinc miracula promat*
> *Antiphaten, Scyllamque & cum Cyclope Charybdin.*

Euoluantur hic fignificatus proprii ex impropriis & in aprico erit regulam in §-propofitam a vate innui, licet cum reftrictione ad primordia.   Caeterum analogam huic regulae notare datur regulam ordinis, quo in mundo fibi res fuccedunt, ad euoluendam creatoris gloriam, fummum & vltimum thema immenfi, liceat ita vocare, poematis.

§. LXXII. Quum fecundum §. 71. coordinatarum repraefentationum quaedam poffint vt praemiffae cum conclufionibus cohaerere, quaedam vt fimile cum fimili & cognatum cum cognato, quaedam per legem fenfationis & imaginationis, *methodus hiftoricorum, ingenii & rationis in lucida poffibilis.*

§. LXXIII. Si regulae methodi vel memoriae vel ingenii contrarientur poeticis e. gr. §. 71. alius vero regulae cum iis conueniant, *ab vna ex iis methodo ad aliam tranfire poeticum* §. II.

Re

Ita interpretamur Flaccum, quando de ordine praecipit, licet haefitabundus

Ordinis haec virtus erit & Venus, aut ego fallor,
Vt iam nunc dicat, iam nunc debentia dici
Pleraque differat & praefens in tempus omittat.

Debentia dici funt, quae methodus vel ingenii, vel memoriae, vel
rationis in antecedentibus obferuata poftularet. Talia *nunc dicit,*
quum enim ordo fit in poemate & methodus, quam aut ipfae aut
ex iis compofitae, vix cogitari queat alia, fecundum aliquam ex iis
vtique connectenda poematis varia; *nunc vero differt,* quia ex alio
cogitationum ordine fuccedentia perfectioni poematis commodio-
ra, adeoque magis poetica. Largimur Horatio diftinctas methodi nec lucidae nec aliarum fu: ffe notiones, nec tamen hinc dubi-
tandum de legitimo fenfu, modo notiones noftrae eadem repraefen-
fentent, licet forte diftinctius. vid. Wolffii I og. lat. § 929.

§. LXXIV. INTRINSECE fiue AESOLVTE
BREVIS eft ORATIO, *cui nihil ineft, quod faluo perfectionis*
gradu abeffe poffet. *Talis breuitas,* quum fit omnis orationis,
eft etiam *poematis* §. 9.

Et tamen πολλα τοι σμικροι λογοι

Εσφηλαν ηδη και κατωρθωσαν βροτες,

Notionem breuitatis eandem animo Horatii haefiffe hariolamur,
quando

Quicquid praecipies efto breuis

cum dixerat, ftatim addit:

Omne fuperuacuum pleno de pectore manat.

Vbi fatis aperte *breuitatem fuperuacuo* opponit. Concipi etiam
poteft ex definitione hac breuitatis, qui fiat vt

breuis effe laborans

Obfcurus fiat.

quum enim ne verbulum quidem redundare velit, cogitationibus
ita orationem refercit, vt fingula non poffint 'a fingulis diftingui,
vnde obfcuritas. Extrinfeca breuitas fiue relatiua non eft ad omnem
neceffaria ordinem, nec ad omne poema, quod fi tamen alicui fpeciei.

eiei peculiaris eſt e. g. epigrammatibus, ex eius affeⅭionibus & de-
terminationibus ſpecificis deducenda eſt.   Cui operae nunc ſubi-
re non eſt animus.

§. LXXV. *Repraeſentationes non poeticae, minusque con-*
nexae cum ſaluo perfeⅭionis poeticae gradu abeſſe poſſint
ex poemate, *eas abeſſe* etiam eſt *poeticum* §. 74. II.

Id eſt, quod more poetico Horatius ſuadet in exemplo Homeri §. 22. quum laudat in eo, quod quae
> *Deſperet traⅭata niteſcere* (extenſiue clariora fieri) *poſſe re*
> *linquat.*

In Ouidii metamorphoſeon libris obſeruabimus quasdam hiſtorias
ſicco prorſus pede tranſeuntem , & vix tribus verbis illarum me-
miniſſe, non ſine luⅭu & indignatione puerorum aniles fabulas
cumulari deſiderantium.

§. LXXVI. Quum quaedam omitti in poemate con-
ſultum §. 75. omnem vero nexum thematis narraturus hiſto-
rici, mirum, quantam mundi partem , ne dixerim , omnem
omnium ſaeculorum hiſtoriam compleⅭi teneatur: *quaedam*
determinantia & remotius connexa omittere poeticum.

Quid Homerus i. e. excellens poeta §. 22. teſte Horatio?
> *Semper ad euentum feſtinat, & in medias res*
> *Non ſecus ac notas auditorem rapit.*

media dicuntur *gemino oue rerum troianarum oppoſita,* quae cohae-
rent, ſed remotius, cum aliis, ita, vt poſſent illa etiam narrari breuitatis non ſtudioſa.   Quae de Homero Flaccus, dicet de Virgilio conſiderans, quomodo res Aeneae incipiat:
> *Vix e conſpeⅭu Siculae telluris in altum &c.*

idem in Comicis plerumque, quorum perſ nae primae etiam , ſi a
prologo diſceſſeris, ita ordiuntur ac ſi totus iam fabulae nexus pa-
teret, quod ob §. 6). apprime vtile.

§. LXXVII. *Voces* cum ad poematis varia pertineant,
§. 10. *debent eſſe poeticae* §. 11. 9.

§. LXXVIII. In vocibus varia 1) *ſonus articulatus,* 2)

D 3

ſigni-

§. XCI. *Voces*,qua soni articulati, pertinent ad audibi ‑
lia, hinc *ideas sensuales producunt.*

§. XCII. *Iudicium de perfectione sensorum confusum* dici‑
tur IVDICIVM SENSVVM, & illi sensorio organo ad‑
scribitur, quod senso afficitur.

Ita exprimere licebit, le gout gallorum, applicatum ad so‑
la sensa. Diiudicationem autem sensibus adscribi et ipsa gallorum
denominatio & Hebraeorum טעם & ריה, & latinorum: loquere,
vt te videam, & Italorum societas del buon gusto, euincunt, ita vt
nonnullae tales loquendi formulae applicentur etiam de distincta
cognitione loquentibus, nolumus tamen eo nunc ascendere; suffi‑
cit non contra vsum sensibus tribui iudicium confusum, & qui‑
dem sensorum.

§. XCIII. *Iudicium* aurium est vel affirmatiuum vel
negatiuum§ 91. affirmatiuum voluptatem, negatiuum tae‑
dium procreabit, quum vtrumque determinet repraesen‑
tatio confusa §. 92. hinc sensitiua §. 3. & poetica §. 12. *excitare
vel taedium vel voluptatem auribus poeticum* §. 11.

§. XCIV. Quo plura consentire vel dissentire notan‑
tur, hoc maius vel taedium, vel voluptas intensior. Iudi‑
cium sensuum omne confusum §. 92. quod si ergo iudicium
A plura consentire vel dissentire obseruet, quam iudicium B,
erit extensiue clarius §. 16. quam B, hinc magis poeticum §.
17. Ergo *summam voluptatem aut summum taedium auribus creare
maxime poeticum.*

§. XCV. Si summum auribus taedium creatur audi‑
toris attentionem auertet, hinc repraesentationes amplius
aut nullae aut paucissimae communicari poterunt, & poema
omni suo fine excidit §. 5. ergo *summam voluptatem auribus
creare poeticum* §. 94.

§. XCVI. Quum *poema* excitet voluptatem aurium, *qua*

series

series sonorum articulatorum §. 92.91. qua tali etiam *inesse de-bet perfectio* §.92. & quidem *summa* §.94.

§. XCVII.   Deduci hinc facile potest poematis necessaria puritas , concinnitas , figurarum ornatus; sed haec ipsi cum imperfecta sensitiua oratione communia facile transimus , pro fine ne nimii simus.   Nihil ergo de qualitate poematis, qua series sonorum articulatorum : cur concursus vocalium, elisiones crebriores, consortium eorundem elementorum vitandum sit.   Omnis *in qualitatibus sonorum articulatorum obuia perfectio* dici posset : SONORI-TAS, termino, nisi fallimur, ex Prisciani schola mutuato.

§. XCVIII. QVANTITAS SYLLABAE est, *quicquid in ea non potest cognosci sine compraesentia alterius sylla-bae.* Ergo *ex moris elementorum non potest cognosci quantitas.*

Placet philologis ebraeis aliquibus tribuere ex morarum elementarium numero aequali aliquam syllabis quantitatem, quae tamen cum hac nostra minime confundenda.   Christianus Rauius Orthographiae ebraeae c. II. §. 17. expressis verbis: *Longitudo &. breuitas syllabae intelligenda hic mere orthographica non prosodica, ne, quis fallatur aut fallat.*   Secundum illam orthographicam, cuius distinctum conceptum suppeditare nostrum nunc prorsus non est, asseritur syllabarum ebraearum aequalitas, secundum hanc, quam definimus poeticam, doceri ea nunquam potest, nisi doceantur falsissima.

§. XCIX.   *Si in loquendo sua cuiuis syllabae tribuitur quantitas,* SCANDITVR.

§. C.   *Si mora syllabae A in scandendo* = *morae sylla-bae B + mora syllabae C, A dicitur longa, C & B breues.*

Mora in grammaticis est pars temporis elemento efferendo necessaria, iam ergo quum de syllabis solum agendum est, mutan-

E   dis

ergo

tas v
tantu
deter
tro,
ex il
cum

ta, e

absol
iam
repr

ritas, concinnitas &c. effe etiam poteft carmen, cui ifta de-
funt, non effe poteft poema per §§. antecedentes & §. 9.
ergo *quoddam carmen non eft poema.*

Hinc iure tam fedulo inter carminificem & poetam diftin-
guunt, & cuculli illi piperis & affae, qui cuduntur quotidie, carmina falutantur, nunquam poemata, plurima quia pars tam augu-
fto rubefceret titulo, charta fi erubefceret, aut parentum impuden-
tia fœtus ipfos non inquinaret.

§. CVI. Paronomafiae finales, quae rythmi nunc
vocantur contra vfum genuinum §. 103. litterarum lufus
in acroftichis, figurarum expreffiones e. g crucis, piri, co-
ni &c. & huius furfuris plura aut apparentes funt perfe-
ctiones, aut determinantur per iudicium aurium certi po-
puli particulare, fimiliter quae lyricum, epicum, drama-
ticum cum fubdiuifis generibus fingularia habent, conuenire quidem debent cum effentialibus perfectionibus, fed
demonftrari non poffunt, nifi ex fpecierum quarumuis
definitionibus determinatioribus. Cantus & actio fiue
recitatio pathetica modi itidem, quum mirifice tamen fa-
ciant ad finem poematis, tanti etiam aeftumati funt veteri-
bus, fuis cancellis inclufi, quos fi erumpunt, vt noftra nunc
theatra excedunt, impediunt potius quam promouent ex
poemate oriundam delectationem. Talia dicta faepius
non dicenda funt iterum.

§. CVII. Quum metrum ideas fenfuales produ-
cat §. 103. 102. eae vero extenfiue clariffimae adeoque maxime magisque poeticae, quam minus clarae §. 17. *metri
leges accuratiffimae obferuari admodum poeticum.* coll. §. 29.

Legiti-

Legitimum debemus fonum digitis & aure callere Plauti-
ni numeri nimium patienter, ne dicam ftulte laudantur, & quanquam noftra praefertim aetate

> *Non quiuis videt immodulata poemata iudex,*
> *Et data Romanis venia eft indigna poetis,*
> *Idcircone vager, fcribamue licenter, an omnes*
> *Vifuros peccata putem mea?*

§. CVIII. IMITARI fi de perfona dicatur, imi-
tatur aliquid, *qui illi fimile producit?* Hinc *effectus fimilis al-
teri* IMITAMEN eius dici poteft, fiue ex intentione, fiue
alia ex cauffa talis factus fit.

§. CIX. Poema, fi imitamen dicatur naturae aut
actionum, effectus effe iubetur fimilis a natura productis.
§. 107.

> *Saltantes Satyros imitabitur Alphefiboeus.*

§. CX. Repraefentationes a natura i. e. intrinfe-
co mutationum in vniuerfo principio, & inde pendentibus
actionibus producendae immediate nunquam diftinctae &
intellectuales, fed fenfitiuae, extenfiue tamen clariffimae
§. 24 16. tales & poeticae §. 9. 17. ergo natura (liceat de
phoenomeno fubftantiato cum actionibus inde pendentibus loqui tanquam de fubftantia) & poeta producunt fimilia §. 26. Hinc *poema* eft *imitamen naturae & actionum inde*
pendentium §. 108.

§. CXI. Si quis *poema* per *orationem ligatam* (carmen §. 104.) *imitamen actionum vel naturae* definiret: duas
notas habet praecipuas per fe inuicem non determinatas,
determinandas ambas ex noftra §. 104. 109. ergo confen-
tientes videmur ad effentiam poematis acceffiffe forfan
propius.

Vid.

Vid. Ariſto:eles de arte poetica C. I.   Vosſius de artis poe-
tieæ natura & conſtitutione c. 4. §. 1. Celeb. IOH. CHRIST.
GOTTSCHEDIVS in arte critica poetica p. 82. 118.

§. CXII.   VIVIDVM dicimus, *in quo plura varia,*
ſeu ſimultanea ſuerint, ſeu ſucceſſiua, *appercipere datur.*

Conferatur definitio cum vſu loquendi, vbi diuerſiſſimis
coloribus illitam piâuram, **ein lebhafftes Gemählde,** eam orationem, quae plura varia appercipienda offert, tam in ſono, quam
ſignatis, **einen lebhafften Vortrag,** conſuetudinem, in qua ſomni
nullus metus ob varias aâiones ſibi continuo ſuccedentes, **einen
lebhafften Umgang** nuncupamus.

§. CXIII.   Si quis cum Vener. ARNOLDO, **in
dem Verſuch einer Syſtematiſchen Einleitung zur teut-
ſchen Poeſie,** poema definiret per *orationem, quae cum obſer-
uatione tonorum* (metro) *rem, quam fieri poteſt, viuidiſſime
repraeſentet. & omni conceptibili vi in animum lectoris ad eum
certo modo commouendum ſe inſinuet,* notas has conſtituit: 1)
metrum, 2) repraeſentationes, quae eſſe poſſunt, viuidiſ-
ſimas, 3) ad commotionem lectoris tendentem aâionem
in animum eius.   Prior determinatur ex noſtra §. 104. 4)
ſunt extenſiue clarae coll. §. 111. & 16. tertia fluit ex noſtra
per §. 25. 26. 27.

§. CXIV.   Definitio poeſeos Ven. WALCHII in
Lexico Philoſ. quod ſit *ſpecies eloquentiae, qua auxilio ingenii* (hoc ſolum non facit poetam) *cogitationes primarias* (themata) *variis ingenioſis & lepidis cogitationibus, aut imaginibus, aut repraeſentationibus veſtimus, ſiue ſoluta ſiue ligata fiat
oratione,* nimis lata, & quae *linguam affectuum* vocat, nimis
anguſta videtur, quae tamen poeſi iure tribuuntur ex noſtra itidem determinabilia.

§.CXIV.

§. CXV. Philosophia poetica est per §.'9. scientia ad perfectionem dirigens orationem sensitiuam. Quum vero in loquendo repraesentationes eas habeamus, quas communicamus, supponit philosophia poetica facultatem in poeta sensitiuam inferiorem. Haec in sensitiue cognoscendis rebus dirigenda quidem esset per Logicam sensu generaliore, sed qui nostram scit logicam, quam incultus hic ager sit, non nesciet. Quid? si ergo, quos arctiores in limites reapse includitur LOGICA etiam per ipsam definitionem in eosdem redigeretur, habita pro *scientia vel philosophice aliquid cognoscendi*, vel *facultatem cognoscitiuam superiorem dirigente in cognoscenda veritate*? Tunc enim daretur occasio philosophis non fine ingenti lucro inquirendi in ea etiam artificia, quibus inferiores cognescendi facultates expoliri possent, acui, & ad emolumentum orbis felicius adhiberi. Quum psychologia det firma principia, nulli dubitamus *scientiam* dari posse *facultatem cognoscitiuam inferiorem, quae dirigat*, aut *scientiam sensitiue quid cognoscendi*.

§. CXVI. Existente definitione, terminus definitus excogitari facile potest, graeci iam philosophi & patres inter αισθητα & νοητα sedulo semper distinxerunt, satisque apparet αισθητα iis non solis aequipollere sensualibus, quum absentia etiam sensa (ergo phantasmata) hoc nomine honorentur. Sunt ergo νοητα cognoscenda facultate superiore obiectum logices, αισθητα επιστημης αισθητικης siue AESTHETICAE.

§. CXVII. Philosophus, vt meditatus, ita proponit, hinc in proponendo nullas aut paucissima peculiares regulae obseruandae. Terminus non erit, qua sunt soni

ni

ni articulati, eatenus enim pertinent ad αισθητα. Horum maiorem habere tenetur rationem fenfitiue proponens, hinc aeftethicae pars de proponendo prolixior effet, quam logicae. Iam quum perfecte hoc fieri poffit & imperfecte, hoc doceret RHETORICA GENERALIS *fcientia de imperfecte repraefentationes fenfitiuas proponendo in genere*, & illud POETICA GENERALIS *fcientia de perfecte proponendo repraefentationes fenfitiuas in genere*. Tam illius in facram & profanam, iudicialem, demonftratiuam, deliberatiuam &c. quam huius in epicam, dramaticam, lyricam cum variis fpeciebus analogis diuifiones relinquerent philofophi harum artium rhetoribus, qui hiftoricam & experimentalem earum cognitionem animis infererent. Ipfi in demonftrandis generalibus & definiendis praefertim accuratis poefeos & eloquentiae pedeftris limitibus occuparentur, quae gradu quidem folo differunt, determinandis tamen quantitatibus huic illiue licitis non minonorem opinamur geometram requirunt, quam Phrygum Myforumque

FINES.